IDENTITY CRISIS

IDENTITY CRISIS

Teaching Imaginary Economics versus Real Economics

Daniel Wentland

ROWMAN & LITTLEFIELD
Lanham • Boulder • New York • London

Published by Rowman & Littlefield
An imprint of The Rowman & Littlefield Publishing Group, Inc.
4501 Forbes Boulevard, Suite 200, Lanham, Maryland 20706
www.rowman.com

6 Tinworth Street, London SE11 5AL

Copyright © 2019 by Daniel Wentland

All rights reserved. No part of this book may be reproduced in any form or by any electronic or mechanical means, including information storage and retrieval systems, without written permission from the publisher, except by a reviewer who may quote passages in a review.

British Library Cataloguing in Publication Information Available

Library of Congress Cataloging-in-Publication Data

Name: Wentland, Daniel M., author.
Title: Identity crisis : teaching imaginary economics versus real economics / Daniel Wentland.
Description: Lanham : Rowman & Littlefield, [2019] | Includes bibliographical references and index.
Identifiers: LCCN 2019013291 (print) | LCCN 2019022369 (ebook) | ISBN 9781475851991 (cloth) | ISBN 9781475852004 (pbk.)
Subjects: LCSH: Economics—Study and teaching. | Economics. | Education—Evaluation.
Classification: LCC HB74.5 .W44 2019 (print) | LCC HB74.5 (ebook) | DDC 330.071—dc23
LC record available at https://lccn.loc.gov/2019013291
LC ebook record available at https://lccn.loc.gov/2019022369

CONTENTS

Introduction: Framing the Issue   vii

PART ONE: THE STARTING POINT   1
1   Questions Not Properly Answered and Educational Reality   3
2   Identity Crisis and Handouts versus a Hand Up   11

PART TWO: SETTING THE FOUNDATION   17
3   Proclaiming the Truth and Two Worldviews   19
4   Which Path to Follow?   27
5   Facts versus Opinions   47
6   Micromanaging Never Works and Useless Politicians versus Useful Politicians   53

PART THREE: THE SCHIZOPHRENIC WORLD OF ECONOMICS AND TEACHING CHOICE IN ECONOMICS EDUCATION   65
7   Economic Way of Thinking   67
8   Imaginary Economics versus Real Economics   75
9   Choice and Economic Education   89

Summary: Concluding the Issue   95
About the Author   99

INTRODUCTION

Framing the Issue

Life is all about decision-making. In fact, the character of each person and the structure of each society are the result of previous decisions. The accumulated impact of decisions shapes the world and determines an individual's position in life.

Several crucial decisions at the societal level include: How does a society develop a child into a productive adult? How does a society determine what goods and services are produced and how those goods and services are produced and distributed? Overlapping these macro-educational and -economic decisions is another fundamental life dilemma that focuses on the limitations of government: Should government control the members of a society, or should the members of a society be in control of the government?

History has clearly demonstrated that government-controlled societies cause economic and social misery. However, despite this realization, the false premise of creating a government-controlled utopian society persists. To shed light on the misguided devotion to government, this book exposes the truths regarding education and economics so that every individual can understand the negative ramifications of implementing policies and practices based on educational and economic falsehoods.

After studying educational theories and economics principles for many years, what troubles me is that the path to a fulfilling life exists, but it is buried under political myths and ideology. The reason misguided political myths and ideologies flourish is that the fundamental principles of education and economics have not been communicated to the public in a persuasive manner, meaning most books contain too much jargon and are too long. In today's fast-paced society, messages must be delivered quickly. Thus, the writing in this book is kept to a minimum so that the positive economic message is clearly communicated.

An economic philosophy predicated on government control, educational policies, and economic-teaching methodologies that disregard economic principles is at the heart of societal failure. For those who ignore this reality, misery will result.

Ultimate Truths

- Societies built on educational and economic falsehoods are doomed to underperform, and the most vulnerable members of society will suffer the most.
- Economic education must promote economic realities, not political ideology.

Part One

The Starting Point

I

QUESTIONS NOT PROPERLY ANSWERED AND EDUCATIONAL REALITY

Questions that are not properly answered do not go away. Many educational questions remain a mystery because we fail to face the reality behind the questions. In other words, we look away from the essential truths that hinder student achievement. As a result, we must ask ourselves the following question: Does society truly want to overcome the problems associated with education, from preschool to graduate programs?

Do we want to improve education?

If the answer to this question is yes, then political crosscurrents and educational ideologies must be peeled away so the reality associated with education and learning can take center stage. Only after we deal with reality can education and learning be maximized. That's the heart of the matter.

Effective school theories are based on the notion that all students will achieve at a high level of learning. This is a myth, and anyone with common sense can clearly see the lack of truthfulness embedded in the notion. Chasing myths is time-consuming and expensive, deflecting resources and priorities away from realistic learning goals and reasonable education policies. As long as education policy continues to be directed toward pie-in-the-sky ideologies, the educational community will continue down an unproductive, destructive path, much like an object approaching the event horizon of a black hole. Once caught in an event horizon, an object cannot escape, so let's move away from myth-chasing and toward reality.

———

Educational policies and practices should not be based on political ideologies but rather educational realities.

———

Reality is reflected in the complexity of learning. Complex tasks tend to be difficult, nonroutine, or novel. Simple tasks tend to be easy, routine, and standard. Despite the difficulty associated with a complex task, all students can learn if they so choose. However, the level of learning will vary. Not all students will earn an A, but all students can increase their knowledge if they put forth the necessary effort.

The two primary reasons that not all students will earn an A are straightforward. The first reason is that not all students are the same. Each student brings a different level of knowledge, skills, abilities, and experiences to the educational setting. Second, there is no guarantee that time and effort will result in accomplishing a complex task. This second reason can be illustrated by Albert Einstein, who, despite being a genius, was never able to finish the complex task of formulating and quantifying a unified field theory. Therefore, even the "smartest among us" may lack the human capital to complete complicated tasks.

DEVELOPING HUMAN CAPITAL

Gary Becker (1964) laid the foundation for the study of human capital acquisition when he distinguished between *general* human capital and *specific* human capital. General human capital has multiple uses and is therefore portable; specific human capital is useful in a narrow line of work and therefore has limited portability. Accordingly, general training is basically an investment in human capital to increase an employee's overall productivity, and it can be transferred to any employment situation. Specific training increases worker productivity only in the job area where the training occurred.

Public education starts the clock in terms of the skills and abilities that future employees will initially bring to the workplace. Therefore, public education has short-term and long-term consequences relating to general and specific human capital development. At the core of human capital development is the learning process.

Based on the work of Bandura (1977), the learning process can be encapsulated in a framework, shown in figure 1.1, that consists of four components:

1. **Attention:** Gaining awareness—focusing on what is being studied
2. **Retention:** Physical and mental ability to acquire new knowledge, skills, abilities, or a combination of these
3. **Reproduction:** Applying new knowledge, skills, abilities, or a combination of these
4. **Motivation:** The desire to learn

The four components of learning can be rearranged to better illustrate the potential level of learning (see figure 1.2). What the four components of learning demonstrate is that the educational environment should be about improving learning outcomes and nothing else.

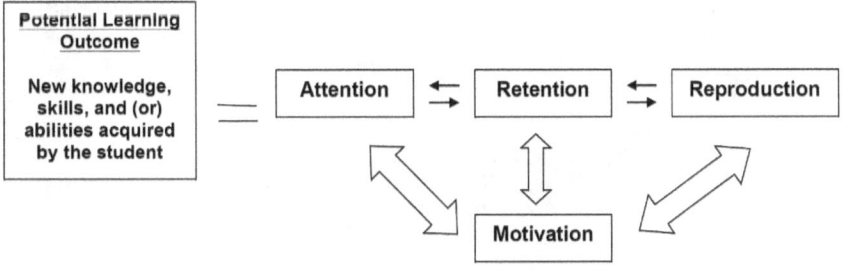

Figure 1.1.

IMPLICATIONS FOR A SCHOOL

The following are some conclusions and recommendations regarding student learning in a school setting:

Reinforce proper actions, behaviors, and statements. Improper actions, behaviors, and statements should be discouraged.

Students learn best when they understand the objective of the educational program. The educational objective should consist of three components: an explanation of what the student is expected to do (performance); a statement of the quality or level of performance that is acceptable (criterion); and a declaration of the conditions under which the student is expected to perform the desired outcome (conditions). In sum, specific objectives or goals must be identified.

Students tend to learn better when the educational experience is linked to their current life situation, future life expectations, or both because this enhances the meaningfulness of the learning situation.

Students are more motivated to learn when they have input in the characteristics of the learning situation, such as course selection and career orientation objectives.

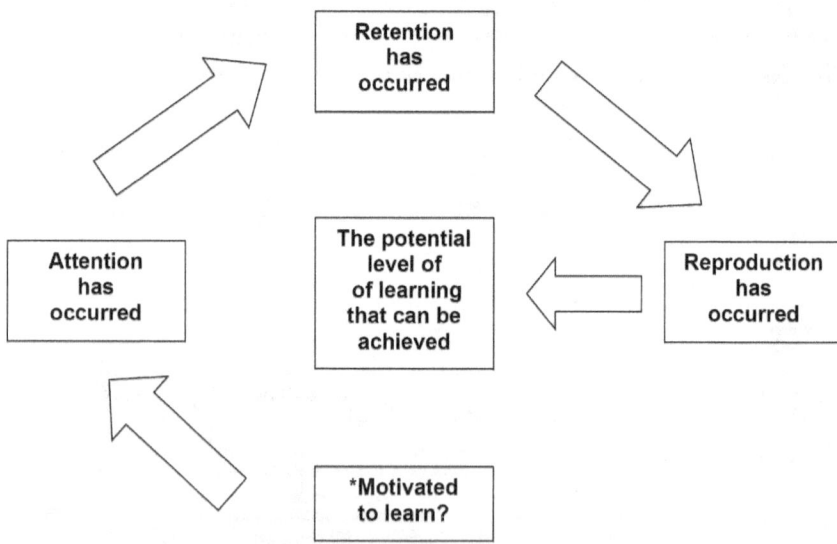

Figure 1.2. *There is a higher probability that motivated students will learn more and at a faster pace.

Students learn best when they have an opportunity to practice. The teacher should identify and explain three things: what the students will be doing when practicing the objectives (performance); the criteria for attainment of the objective; and the conditions under which the practice session(s) will be conducted. The educational experience might be further enhanced by providing students with opportunities to choose their practice strategies.

Students need feedback. To be effective, the feedback should be specific and provided as soon as possible.

Students learn by observing and imitating a technique or model. For a technique or model to be effective, the desired solution, behaviors, or skills must be clearly specified. After observing the technique or model, students should have the opportunity to reproduce the technique or imitate the skills and behaviors illustrated by the model.

Students need the curriculum and classroom to be properly coordinated and arranged. Good coordination ensures that students are not distracted by an uncomfortable room, poorly organized materials, or anything else that might interfere with learning.

The best learning environment is a place that is comfortable, accessible, quiet, and private, with enough space, equipment, and supplies. Additional room considerations should include:

1. Checking for noise from heating and air conditioning systems, adjacent rooms or corridors, and sources outside the building.
2. Pastel colors tend to be warm. White and beige are cold and sterile, while blacks and browns appear to "close up" the room and can create fatigue.
3. Long and narrow rooms make it difficult to see and hear. Try to select a somewhat square room.
4. Fluorescent lights should be the main source of lighting, but incandescent lighting should be spread throughout the room and controlled with a dimmer switch when projection is required.
5. Solid-color carpeting should be placed in the room.
6. Chairs should be comfortable, with backs that support the lower lumbar region. Chairs with wheels that swivel are preferred.
7. Higher ceilings are preferred to lower ceilings (ten-foot ceilings are recommended).

8. Ample electrical outlets and computer and telephone jacks should be placed throughout the room.
9. Monitor voice clarity and level throughout the room.
10. Eliminate glare from metal surfaces, TVs, and computer monitors.

Learning is most likely to occur when a student believes that his or her effort will lead to a desired outcome. It is important that the outcome is valued by the student so that the student will be motivated to achieve the learning outcome.

Student learning can be enhanced if the teacher keeps the attention of the students focused on what is being modeled or studied. The teacher should understand how incentives and motivational processes can positively or negatively influence retention and reproduction.

To conclude, learning is the formal or informal process of acquiring new knowledge, skills, or abilities. Knowledge can be defined as remembering previously learned information, such as facts, terms, procedures, and principles. The accumulation of knowledge, skills, and abilities requires time, persistence, and effort. This is the ultimate reality regarding education and learning. Those students who do not acknowledge this truth will lack a realistic view of what it takes to succeed academically. Educators who do not inform their students of this educational and learning reality are doing a great disservice to their students.

SUMMARY

- Chasing educational myths diverts scarce resources away from realistic educational policies and practices.
- Public education has short-term and long-term consequences relating to general and specific human capital development. At the core of human capital development is learning.
- Learning is the formal or informal process of acquiring new knowledge, skills, or abilities, and the learning process consists of four components: attention, retention, reproduction, and motivation.
- The accumulation of knowledge, skills, and abilities requires time, persistence, and effort. This is the ultimate reality regarding education and learning.

REFERENCES

Bandura, A. (1977). *Social learning theory*. Upper Saddle River, NJ: Prentice-Hall.
Becker, G. (1964). *Human capital*. New York: Columbia University Press.

2

IDENTITY CRISIS AND HANDOUTS VERSUS A HAND UP

As previously stated, questions that are not properly answered will not go away. Solutions to educational questions remain a mystery because it is easier to hide from the realities of learning, education, and student achievement than to confront them openly and honestly.

―ɷɷ―

It might not be politically correct to tell it like it is; however, if we want to move from the shadows and into the light of sustainable student achievement, then we can no longer afford to look away from the mirror of educational truth.

―ɷɷ―

In the previous chapter, a fundamental reality of learning and education started the process of moving toward the light by highlighting a fact associated with student achievement. No sugarcoating, just the truth. Learning is a complex task that requires time, persistence, and effort. For those students who refuse to work extremely hard, the probability of academic success is unlikely.

Realizing that many educators and policy makers do not want to accept the facts regarding education helps to explain why the underrealization of human potential is so often a product of public education. When one doesn't face reality, then problems are bound to follow.

UNDERREALIZATION VERSUS REALIZATION OF HUMAN POTENTIAL

There can be no greater task than to extinguish the underrealization of human potential. Why are schools not the place where the human potential of all students can be realized? Why has education been turned upside down and inside out by the fostering of the underrealization of human potential instead of the realization of human potential?

The upside-down, inside-out learning situation in most educational settings is a primary criticism haunting public education, and given the many fads, ideologies, theories, economic agendas, political crosscurrents, and unexamined assumptions associated with education, it's no wonder that educational results have been mixed.

Navigating the world of education is like sailing on a rudderless boat and being blown by the wind in one direction and then another. You might travel a long distance, but you most likely will never arrive at your intended destination. The loss of direction in education can be traced to the confusion over what it is supposed to be, how it is best achieved, and the obstacles that must be overcome to do so.

———∽∾∽———

Education has lost focus and direction.

———∽∾∽———

Several educational ideologies have emerged: perennialism, essentialism, progressivism, critical theory, multicultural education, constructivism, and objectivism. Each provides an alternative approach for understanding the role of education. For example, according to the educational theory of perennialism, important truths do not change over time. Educational programs should focus on unchanging principles, and vocational training should not be emphasized.

Essentialism suggests there is a core of essential knowledge primarily derived from scientific and technical fields that must be mastered by all students. Essentially, the most valued knowledge is that which is practical and useful.

Progressivism is a philosophy that views change as the essence of reality and promotes the view that schools should develop learners' problem-solving skills to help students cope with change.

Critical theory is a contemporary extension of social reconstructionism. This theory of education advocates using schools to engineer a new society and transform existing social inequalities and injustices.

Multicultural education seeks educational equity for all students by requiring a curriculum that accurately illustrates how various cultures have influenced Western civilization.

Constructivism suggests that students control their learning. A major belief of constructivism is that knowledge is subjective and relative to the individual or community. Constructivism is an approach to learning in which students construct new understandings through active engagement with their past and present experiences.

Objectivism asserts that knowledge has an independent existence and emphasizes knowledge absorption by passive learners.

Summarized here are additional interpretations of what education is:

- In the early history of public education, developing good character was considered essential. The emphasis on developing good character is a recurring cycle in educational literature.
- The key to success in education depends on a commitment to a broad curriculum, with an emphasis on liberal arts and the sciences. In contrast, other educational scholars place an emphasis on improving student reading and math outcomes.
- In some educational circles, academic content is the primary focus, while other researchers stress that learning how to think critically is the path to better educational outcomes.
- The primary purpose of public education is economic, which means that the objective should be to prepare students to compete in the global economy. Other educational theorists state that the major purpose of public education is to prepare students to participate effectively as citizens.
- Some educators suggest that education policy should be based on the following five requirements:

    1. National content standards
    2. Standardized test scores

3. Highly qualified teachers in every classroom
4. The requirement of all students to take math courses throughout high school
5. A reduction in the student dropout rate by ending social promotion and funding dropout-prevention programs

- Education is associated with doing well academically and achieving good grades on examinations. Other definitions of *education* assert that quality education consists of developing students who respect other people.
- Competency-based education (CBE) reflects the "ability to do something" rather than earning high grades on examinations.
- *Education* has been defined as a social system that should deliver quality instruction to the students.
- The purpose of education is to promote social, emotional, and mental growth versus traditional intellectual development.
- Various approaches to teaching should include: (1) devising and using instructional objectives that specify observable, measurable student behaviors; (2) a behavioral approach (direct instruction) focusing on learning basic skills, with the teacher making all decisions, keeping students on task, and emphasizing positive reinforcement; (3) a cognitive approach facilitating meaningful learning, in which students discover how to be autonomous, self-directed learners; (4) a humanistic approach that pays attention to student needs, emotions, values, and self-perceptions; and (5) a social approach stressing how students can learn from each other.

What can be gleaned from the array of confusing ideologies and definitions of education?

With the various educational philosophies, theories, assumptions, and viewpoints, what becomes clear is that the basic role of education has been lost. However, this loss of identity also provides a path for educational improvement. As stated by Paul Davies (1988), "The fact that the universe is full of complexity does not mean that the underlying laws are also complex." The same reasoning can be applied to education.

To improve educational outcomes, the time has come for educational scholars, practitioners, and policy makers to agree on a definition of *education* and its role in society. To begin clarifying the role of education, the following statements are offered:

1. Formal education is a structured system (process and environment) in which learning occurs. *Learning* is defined as acquiring new knowledge, skills, abilities, or a combination of these.
2. The purpose of formal education is to maximize the learning environment.
3. To accomplish the purpose of formal education, the realities associated with learning and education must be acknowledged, and educational decisions must be driven by those realities, not political ideology.

If educational scholars, practitioners, and policy makers do not eliminate the confusion over the role of education, then the underrealization of human potential will continue to be the end product of the educational process.

Economic education is in a state of confusion because, like the field of education, economic education suffers from an identity crisis. There is a difference between the mind-set that embraces the ideology that big government and a never-ending list of social programs can promote individual prosperity and the philosophy that focuses on fostering an economic environment where energic individuals have an opportunity to be productive and achieve a high standard of living.

Distributing economic handouts through political programs is not an effective way to help an individual live a fulfilling life; it only creates government dependency. And make no mistake about it: dependency on the government is the desired outcome of the politicians and economists who promote imaginary economics. Government control over the individual is the goal of imaginary economics. In contrast, real economics focuses on the realization that providing an economic hand up is the only way to establish an economic and social environment where individuals are free to pursue their dreams and help others achieve a fulfilling life.

Uncovering the difference between imaginary economics and real economics is important because, when it's all said and done, what can be more compelling in life than helping individuals build a better future? The information in this book will open your eyes so that the truth can be seen.

A government distributing economic handouts or one providing an economic hand up? The economic distinction between the two choices is clear: government handouts and dependency versus an economic hand-up and self-fulfillment. It's time to stop the political foolishness and get on with the work of truly helping everyone succeed.

SUMMARY

- An identity crisis in education has developed because of the various viewpoints regarding the definition and role of education. However, like the phoenix rising from the ashes, it is the loss of identity that provides an opportunity to improve education.
- If educational scholars, practitioners, and policy makers do not eliminate the confusion over the role of education, then the underrealization of human potential will continue to be the end product of the educational process.
- The identity crisis in economic education stems from the confusion in economics over the optimal approach to helping individuals achieve a fulfilling life—through the political ideology of imaginary economics or the principles of real economics.

REFERENCE

Davies, P. (1988). *The cosmic blueprint: New discoveries in nature's creative ability to order the universe*. New York: Touchstone Books.

Part Two

Setting the Foundation

3

PROCLAIMING THE TRUTH AND TWO WORLDVIEWS

Unfortunately, the political correctness (PC) crowd who practices imaginary economics has created a situation where the myths of the ideology are believed to be reality, and that perceived reality has snared many victims, like the deadly tentacles of an octopus. Once an individual is captured and accepts the falsehoods of imaginary economics, it's next to impossible to avoid a lifetime of economic stagnation.

―∽∽―

Repeating myths can lead some individuals to believe that the myths are reality.

―∽∽―

As more and more people are caught in the downward economic spiral of imaginary economics, society will eventually reach a tipping point where nothing can be reversed, like an object approaching the event horizon of a black hole. Once past the event horizon, it's over for the object, and so it will be for the society. In the end, imaginary economics destroys the society, leaving in its wake chaos and misery. Economic desperation and minimal living standards will become the norm.

CHAPTER 3

—∽∽—

The policies of imaginary economics create misery.

—∽∽—

The only way to avoid the endgame of imaginary economics is to promote and embrace the reality of real economics. The societal choice between imaginary economics and real economics is what determines whether people will have an opportunity to live a fulfilling life.

—∽∽—

The principles of real economics will lead to a fulfilling life and better economic opportunities for all.

—∽∽—

In the final analysis, everyone's life will be profoundly affected by the number of people who can recognize and debunk the falsehoods of imaginary economics and its misguided and delusional promises. For those who truly want to achieve a rewarding life for themselves and others, please read on to uncover the pie-in-the-sky falsehoods of imaginary economics and discover the economic prowess of real economics.

Exposing the social and economic misery caused by the economists, politicians, reporters, academicians, and the other followers who perpetuate the myths of imaginary economics is the most crucial economic task facing society because the difference between imaginary and real economics is prosperity for all.

—∽∽—

Cutting through the misleading policies and practices of imaginary economics while highlighting the economic reality of true economics is the only way to help everyone succeed.

—∽∽—

INTENTIONS WORLDVIEW VERSUS RESULTS-ORIENTED WORLDVIEW

The truth about economics is that the field consists of individuals who view the world from two mutually exclusive perspectives. One of the worldviews focuses on intentions of social policies and programs; the other viewpoint is centered on the actual results of the policies and programs.

Two Economic Worldviews

Intentions Worldview
Results-Oriented Worldview

The intentions worldview is a mirage and only exists in the minds of those economists and individuals who generally forget the principles of the economic way of thinking. The "intentions practitioners" generally brush aside the outcomes of social policies and programs because the outcomes rarely match the intentions. It's sad but true that many innocent people have been deceived by the intentions worldview because everything that is proposed sounds so good. Unfortunately, economic stagnation is what follows when the principles of economics are ignored and the societal utopia promised by practitioners of the intentions worldview never materializes. Poverty and despair are most often the result for those individuals who surrender to the policies and promises of the so-called intellectuals and others in society who proclaim the intentions worldview.

The intentions worldview of economics is a mirage because intentions rarely match outcomes.

The bottom line is that facts and reality must be ignored by the economists, politicians, reporters, teachers, academicians, and the other followers who believe in the intentions worldview. Nothing is more important to the promoters, implementers, and followers of the intentions worldview than the survival of their government-focused ideology. The ideology must survive at any personal or societal cost. The ideology becomes their religion. Nothing must stand in the way of the ideology, especially the facts. Those who foster the intentions worldview are economic imposters who, like Captain Edward Smith, will lead all who follow them toward a societal and economic iceberg; we know the result of the *Titanic* tragedy.

The supporters of the intentions worldview ignore reality and are economic imposters.

In contrast, the results-oriented worldview focuses on the economic outcomes of social policies and programs. The logic is straightforward: If the outcomes of a social program do not match the intentions, then the social program and its policies must be eliminated or altered so that intentions and outcomes are in line with each other.

The Results-Oriented Worldview
The intentions of a social program must match the outcomes of the program.

The results-oriented viewpoint can be encapsulated by paraphrasing two ideas: one from Milton Friedman, the other from Albert Einstein. First, from Friedman, one of our great mistakes is to judge public policies and programs by the intentions rather than the outcomes. The idea from Einstein deals with the notion of insanity and goes something like this: The ultimate form of insanity is to keep trying the same thing over and over and expecting different results.

The ideas from Friedman and Einstein guide the implementers and followers of the results-oriented worldview. Clearly, the followers of the intentions worldview are forced to look the other way when confronted by the reality of the ideas from Friedman and Einstein because these ideas invalidate their government-focused ideology.

The results-oriented worldview is guided by Milton Friedman's principle regarding intentions versus outcomes and Albert Einstein's definition of insanity.

The distinction between the intentions worldview and the results-oriented worldview forms the dividing line between imaginary economics and real economics, much like a mountain range separates the land on either side of the towering, rocky peaks. Understanding the difference between these two economic philosophies is crucial if society is going to be able to see through the economic smokescreen and the false promises of those economists, politicians, reporters, teachers, academicians, and other followers who spout the misleading rhetoric of the intentions worldview.

The intentions worldview of economics is illusionary, and the economists who preach this ideology are like magicians who make a living by skillfully deceiving the audience into believing that the magician is capable of defying reality. Magicians always put on a great show, and in the end, the crowd enjoys an evening of exciting entertainment. However, for those individuals sucked into the shell game of imaginary economics, the show generally has a bad ending.

The individuals sucked into the intentions worldview of economics generally never escape the false promises of imaginary economics—a government-focused ideology. As their lives crumble and they live in social and economic despair, they become envious of others.

To continue to uncover the falsehoods of imaginary economics, many of the remaining chapters of this book are organized so that the distinction between imaginary economics and real economics becomes more visible. That visibility is what makes this book a must-read for those individuals who truly want to help the less fortunate and make sure that economic education is centered on the principles of real economics.

Recall the parable associated with Jesus about giving a man a fish that feeds him for a day versus teaching a man to fish so that he will have the ability to eat for a lifetime. Imaginary economics (a focus on the intentions of economic and social programs and polices) is about giving a man a fish; real economics (a focus on facts and the actual outcomes of economic and social programs and policies) is about teaching a man to fish. Which economic perspective is the most compassionate?

Which is the most compassionate? Giving a person a fish so he or she can eat for a day or teaching a person to fish so he or she can eat for a lifetime?

It's time for the economists, politicians, reporters, teachers, academicians, and the other followers of the real economics to step up to the plate and stop standing around, watching many individuals fall prey to the false narratives of imaginary economics. We have a lot of work to do, and with so many caught up in the web of imaginary economics, it's time to get going and spread the word that the promises and practices of imaginary economics are pathways to dependency on the government and nothing else.

ECONOMIC EDUCATION AND SPREADING THE WORD

The best method for spreading the word about the devastating consequences of imaginary economics and the beneficial results of real economics is communicating the information in classrooms where economics is taught. Economic education teachers must decide to focus on economic reality by stressing the principles of the economic way of thinking. Real economics is based on the economic way of thinking, while imaginary economics ignores the real-world analysis encapsulated in the economic way of thinking. As the falsehoods of imaginary economics continue to be presented to the public, the reality of real economics will continue to be hidden from public view. Time is of the essence; the teachers of economic education must peel back the illusory promises of imaginary economics.

SUMMARY

- Imaginary economics focuses on the intentions of economic and social programs and policies. Imaginary economics is a false narrative that consists of a series of economic fairy tales. Unfortunately for most individuals, the story has a bad ending.
- Real economics focuses on facts and the actual results of economic and social programs and policies. Real economics is the answer for helping the less fortunate because it's based on reality and its roots are embedded in the basic principles of the economic way of thinking.
- The time for communicating the benefits of real economics is now, before it's too late for all of us!
- Teachers of economic education must communicate the principles of real economics and expose the falsehoods of imaginary economics.

REFERENCE

Friedman, M. (1975, December 7). Interview with Richard Heffner on *The Open Mind*.

4

WHICH PATH TO FOLLOW?

Given today's rapidly changing demographic environment, cultural values and beliefs play a central role in modifying human behavior. To put it simply, the cultural background and life experiences of a person influence their perception of their capability to handle a situation or task.

Culture affects behavior.

In other words, culture affects a person's self-efficacy. A person with high levels of self-efficacy tends to do what is necessary to learn the information and acquire the skills to accomplish a task or goal. However, individuals with low levels of self-efficacy tend to select performance-avoidance goals, which involve reducing the possibility of failure by avoiding novel and challenging tasks and goals. In addition, individuals with low levels of self-efficacy may engage in self-handicapping behaviors and tend to blame performance outcomes on circumstances rather than on their abilities. The bottom line is that individuals with high levels of self-efficacy expect positive outcomes and attribute outcomes to their own abilities and efforts; the opposite is true for individuals with low levels of self-efficacy.

Acknowledging the link between culture, life experiences, self-efficacy, behavior, and outcomes leads to the realization that we must look inward to understand a person's situation in life. Only after we examine and unmask who we really are, are we able to see the life path we have followed.

Unfortunately, gaining a "true" sense of who we are can pose a significant challenge because, at the individual level, it's quite rare to find genuine self-exploration:

> When people turn their psychological insight-apparatus on themselves . . . the brain hangs. The thought process goes and goes, but it doesn't get anywhere. It must be something like that, because we know that people can think about themselves indefinitely. Some people think of little else. Yet people never seem to change as a result of their intensive introspection. They never understand themselves better. . . . It's almost as if you need someone else to tell you who you are, or to hold up the mirror for you. . . . You have to start seeing things as they really are, and not as you want them to be. (Crichton, 2002, 77–78)

Seeing who we really are requires a thorough internal analysis that can lead to an understanding of behavior. Behavior is based on an individual's perception of a situation; their personality; environmental factors, including culture and life experiences; their attitudes; and motivational influences. When combined, each of these variables accounts for our individual differences and behaviors—just like when the various ingredients in a recipe are mixed together to form a meal.

People differ in many ways: perception, personality, environmental factors, attitudes, and motivational influences.

A journey toward uncovering the self reveals what lurks beneath a person's life situation. In fact, understanding our inner self is like the unseen portion of an iceberg that lies below the waterline, and it is what lies beneath the waterline that can be extremely dangerous; the ill-fated voyage of the *Titanic* always serves to remind us of that.

Every minute we spend on this planet defines who we are, why we behave the way we do, and how our actions have affected our successes and failures in life.

An interesting peek into the behavior of the first president of the United States was illustrated in an exhibition titled *Treasures from Mount Vernon: George Washington Revealed* at the New-York Historical Society building in New York City. While wandering around the numerous displays of documents, clothing, pictures, furniture, and a miniature model of Mount Vernon, I stumbled on a letter written by an individual who wrote, "I have attended many occasions at Mount Vernon and have noticed that Mr. Washington rarely speaks and when he does it is never about himself"—a revealing observation of one person on the inner being of another.

Unmasking our inner being, the self beneath the shell of our body, involves an analysis of perception, personality, attitudes, and motivational influences.

Perception is the selection and organization of environmental stimuli to provide meaningful experiences for the perceiver. It involves searching for, obtaining, and processing information. Perception represents the psychological process whereby people take information from the environment and make sense of their worlds.

How we perceive our environment is influenced by internal and external factors. Internal perception factors include attitudes, motives, interests, personality, learning experiences, cultural background, and expectations. Each of these factors is an aspect of the person (or perceiver)—the individual looking at a target and interpreting what he or she sees.

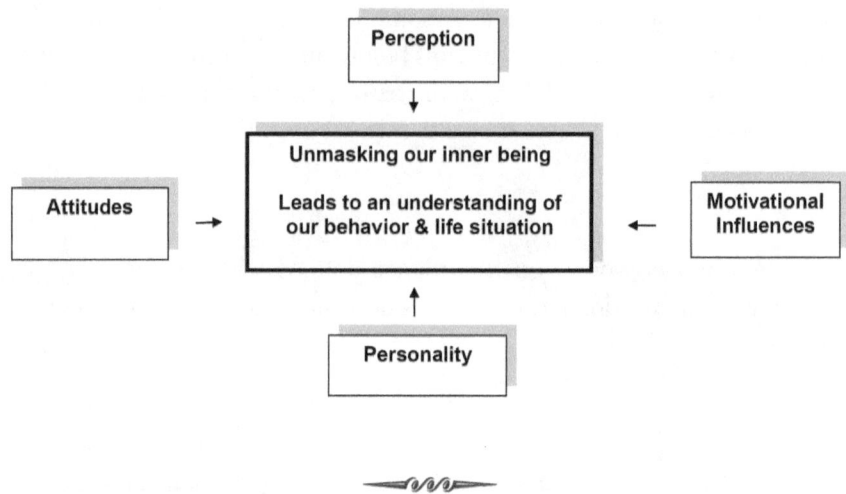

Internal factors are characteristics of the person.

EXTERNAL PERCEPTION FACTORS

Characteristics in the Target

Size. The larger the size, the more likely the factor will be perceived.

Intensity. The more intense (bright lights, loud noises, intensity of writing), the more likely the factor will be perceived.

Background (Contrast). Factors that stand out against a background (or factors that are not what people expect) are more likely to be perceived.

Motion. A moving factor is more likely to be perceived.

Repetition. A repeated factor is more likely to be perceived.

Novelty or Familiarity. Either a familiar or a novel factor in an environment attracts attention, depending on the circumstances.

Proximity. Objects that are close to each other tend to be perceived together rather than separately. As a result of physical or time proximity, we often put together objects or events that are unrelated.

Characteristics of the Situation

Time. The time of day can influence what might be perceived.
Work Setting. Under a particular set of circumstances, a particular work setting might increase the chances of something being noticed and influencing our perception.
Social Setting. Under a particular set of circumstances, a particular social setting might increase the chances of something being noticed and influencing our perception.

External factors are characteristics that influence whether a stimulus is noticed. For our purposes, a "stimulus" can be referred to as any environmental event that may produce a response in an organism. External perception factors include characteristics in the target—what is being perceived (observed) and the situation—characteristics in the immediate environment that influence our perception.

To illustrate the importance of perception, let's consider a thought experiment that Albert Einstein used when developing his theories of special and general relativity. The thought experiment grappled with the question of whether two individuals would see two lightning bolts (traveling at an identical speed and distance) strike two poles at the same time if one of the individuals was in a moving train while the other was standing halfway between the two poles. Both individuals would be holding a specially designed mirror that would allow each of them to continually see the lightning as well as the two poles.

Given this set-up, the experiment provided a theoretical methodology for evaluating whether two individuals witnessing the same event would see the same thing (the same reality). Using common sense, we probably would predict that the two individuals would see the lightning bolts strike the poles at the same time because each of the bolts of lightning would be traveling at the same speed and distance toward the poles. Unfortunately, that evaluation leads us to an incorrect conclusion; the individual positioned in the moving train would first see the lightning strike the pole in the direction that the train was heading and then witness the other pole being struck. The person standing halfway between the two poles would see the lightning bolts strike the poles at the same time.

For us, the story illustrates the notion of perception and how two individuals observing the same situation (environment) may not see the same thing. This creates a problem when we are trying to objectively examine our inner being and the environment in which we live.

Perception and Reality

Perception bends and twists reality via two sources. The first source relates to the previously outlined internal and external perception factors. The second source (referred to as the *self-serving bias*) focuses on our tendency as human beings to attribute our successes to internal factors while placing the blame for failures on external factors. In other words, when we succeed at something, our perception is that the success was achieved primarily because of our efforts, while at the other end of the spectrum, our failures and disappointments are perceived as occurring because of outside forces not under our control.

The self-serving bias allows us to mentally "pass the buck" regarding our actions and provides a convenient outlet for not taking responsibility for our decisions, which when left unchecked can lead to a complete divorce from what actually transpired. This separation from reality forms an effective barrier to honest and sincere self-analysis—an analysis that must occur because we need to understand who we are and how our behavior and actions influence situational outcomes.

Given the illusionary barriers that are erected because of an individual's perception, how can we pull back the veil of misperception to objectively see who we are and how we influence the environment around us? No easy answer exists, but an examination of the attribution process provides some guidance.

The Attribution Process

The attribution process refers to the ways in which people come to understand the causes of others' (and their own) behaviors. Attributions play an important role in perception. Those made about the reasons for someone's behavior may affect judgments about that individual's fundamental characteristics (what he or she is really like).

In the end, the relationship between attributions and an individual's perception of success or failure are linked to four causal factors: ability, effort, task difficulty, and luck. Causal attributions of ability and effort are internal (under the direct control of the individual), while causal attributions of task difficulty and luck are external (not under the direct control of the individual).

INTERNAL ATTRIBUTIONS

Under the Direct Control of the Individual

- I succeeded (or failed) because I had the skills to do the job (or because I did not have the skills to do the job). Such statements are ability attributions.
- I succeeded (or failed) because I worked hard (or because I did not work hard). Such statements are effort attributions.

Not under the Direct Control of the Individual

- I succeeded (or failed) because it was easy (or because it was too hard). Such statements are attributions about task difficulty.
- I succeeded (or failed) because I was lucky (or unlucky). Such statements are attributions about luck or the circumstances surrounding the task.

The four causal factors of success or failure not only play a pivotal role in analyzing how perception might blur reality, but also, more importantly, they provide an individual with a mechanism for gaining insight into his or her behavior and actions. The more individuals understand their own behavior and actions, the further they can walk down the path toward unmasking who they really are.

Lacking an objective analysis of a situation, perception can cloud our judgment, skew our notion of reality, and warp our understanding of who we really are. To burrow beneath the flesh and bones that form our physical image, we need to take an objective look into our spirit or soul. As the misunderstood hero in the movie *Shrek* stated to his donkey companion during their journey to rescue the princess, "an ogre has many layers," and it's time for us to peel back the layers that cover our personality—the core of our being.

The next leg in our voyage of self-discovery will plunge us into a deeper understanding of who we really are by examining the basics of personality.

Personality can be referred to as consistency in behavior and how we react to events and situations. Debate continues on the degree to which our personality is determined by nature (heredity and genetics) or nur-

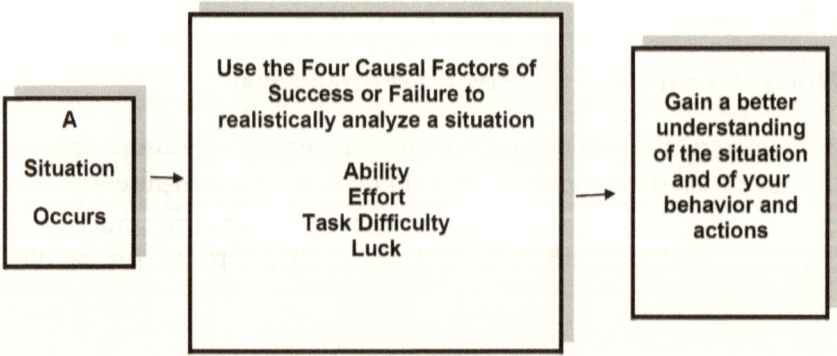

ture (environmental factors, such as culture, family, group membership, and life experiences). In addition to these two factors, a third dimension of personality focuses on the interplay between the situation and the individual.

Although personalities tends to be stable and consistent, under different situations, specific aspects of individual personalities can dominate people's behaviors. For example, a nonviolent individual placed in a life-threatening situation will probably become quite violent. These three dimensions of personality (heredity, nurture, and the situation) form a complex web that drives our behavior and provides important clues to our inner being—the true entity that exists within the walls of our flesh.

Like flowers blossoming on a vine, the various theories to explain our behavior stem from the three dimensions of personality. These theories increase the body of knowledge regarding personality—an intellectual expansion that ultimately moves us closer to understanding ourselves. The theories of personality can generally be divided along two broad schools of thought: descriptive theories and developmental theories.

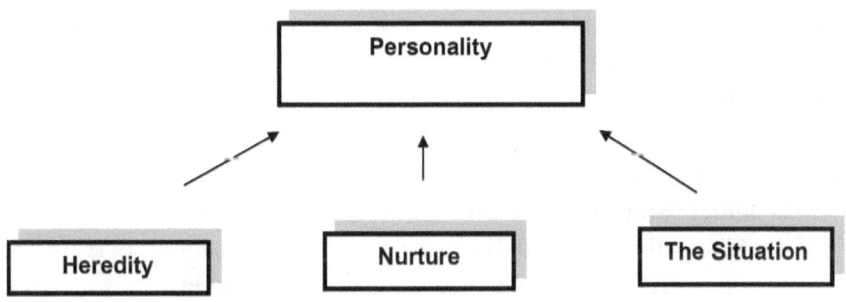

PERSONALITY THEORIES

Descriptive Theories

Type theories classify people into a certain personality type (type A and type B, Myers-Briggs Type Indicator, and internalizers and externalizers).

Trait theories are enduring characteristics or tendencies that describe an individual's behavior (sixteen primary traits, the "big five" personality factors).

Developmental Theories

Psychoanalytic theories of personality development tend to portray human motivation as self-interested and uncivilized unless socially acceptable roles and outlets are provided.

Humanistic theories assume that human nature is essentially positive, productive, and growth-oriented, and that people would develop in healthy ways if they knew how.

Learning theories apply basic principles of learning to the development and function of personality.

TYPE THEORIES

An individual with a type A personality tends to be impatient, is concerned with time and punctuality, is very competitive, is obsessed with numbers, measures success in terms of money or how much they acquire, and strives to think or do two or more things at once. A type B individual tends to be more relaxed, takes one thing at a time, expresses feelings, doesn't suffer from a sense of urgency, feels no need to display or discuss either achievements or accomplishments unless such exposure is demanded by the situation, and can relax without guilt.

The Myers-Briggs Type Indicator is a self-assessment personality test that characterizes an individual along four dimensions.

THE FOUR PERSONALITY DIMENSIONS OR TYPES

Problem-Solving Dimension

The **introverted** person is shy and withdrawn, likes a quiet environment for concentration, dislikes interruptions, and is content to work alone.

The **extroverted** person is outgoing, often aggressive, likes variety, likes to function in a social environment, often acts quickly without thinking, and may dominate situations or people.

Information-Gathering Dimension

Sensing types like action and focus on getting things done; they work steadily and reach a conclusion step by step.

Intuitive types dislike doing the same thing repeatedly, enjoy learning new skills, may arrive at a conclusion quickly, and often follow their inspirations and hunches.

Decision-Making Dimensions

Thinking types excel at putting things in logical order, respond more to people's ideas than feelings, need to be treated fairly, and tend to be firm and tough-minded.

Feeling types like harmony; respond to an individual's values, feelings, and thoughts; tend to be sympathetic; and enjoy pleasing people.

Evaluating Dimensions

Judgment types like to get things finished and work best with a plan; they dislike interrupting their projects and tasks and use lists as agendas.

Perception types adapt well to changing situations and do not mind last-minute changes; they may begin many projects but have difficulty completing them or may postpone unpleasant tasks.

Another personality type framework centers on the terms *introvert* and *extrovert*. Introverts believes they control their own lives and are primarily responsible for what occurs in them. Extroverts perceive that forces outside their own control determine their fates.

TRAIT THEORIES

The sixteen primary traits model of personality classifies human behavior among sixteen traits. According to this theory, an individual displays these traits in a consistent manner, so the traits tentatively provide an explanation of a person's behavior:

1. Reserved vs. Outgoing
2. Less Intelligent vs. More Intelligent
3. Affected by Feelings vs. Emotionally Stable
4. Submissive vs. Dominant
5. Serious vs. Happy-Go-Lucky
6. Expedient vs. Conscientious
7. Timid vs. Venturesome
8. Tough-Minded vs. Sensitive
9. Trusting vs. Suspicious
10. Practical vs. Imaginative
11. Forthright vs. Shrewd
12. Self-Assured vs. Apprehensive
13. Conservative vs. Experimenting
14. Group-Dependent vs. Self-Sufficient
15. Uncontrolled vs. Controlled
16. Relaxed vs. Tense

The "big five" personality factors reduce the number of traits to explain behavior. According to this theory, an individual's personality is encapsulated along a continuum of five primary factors (adjustment, sociability, conscientiousness, agreeableness, and intellectual openness).

PSYCHOANALYTIC THEORIES

Like the roots of a plant reaching deep into the soil to bring forth the nutrients required for life, the foundation for most psychoanalytic theories is grounded in the ideas of Sigmund Freud (1856–1939). According to Freud, the individual at birth has no personality or public persona. An individual's personality (ego) is formed by the interaction between one's superego and the primal urges of the id. The ego abides by the

The "Big Five" Personality Factors
Adjustment   (Stable, confident, effective) - (Nervous, self-doubting, moody)
Sociability   (Gregarious, energetic, self-dramatizing) - (Shy, unassertive, withdrawn)
Conscientiousness   (Plan, neat, dependable) - (Impulsive, careless, irresponsible)
Agreeableness   (Warm, tactful, considerate) - (Independent, cold, rude)
Intellectual Openness   (Imaginative, curious, original) - (Dull, unimaginative, literal-minded)

reality principle, compromising some of the id's demands while not violating too many of the superego's constraints.

HUMANISTIC THEORIES

According to William James (1842–1910), an individual's personality consists of four "selves":

1. Material self: one's physical body and material possessions
2. Social self: how one is viewed by others
3. Spiritual self: one's spiritual thoughts and beliefs
4. Psychological faculties: reasoning; feeling; and the pure ego, maintained in one's ongoing awareness or stream of consciousness

LEARNING THEORIES

Several learning theories provide a foundation for understanding how an individual is motivated to learn and how the learning experience molds one's personality and behavior:

- Reinforcement theory: People are motivated to perform or avoid certain behaviors because of past outcomes that have resulted from those behaviors.
- Social learning theory: Individuals first watch others, who act as models, and then behave according to what they have witnessed.
- Goal setting theory: Establishing and committing to specific, challenging goals can influence an individual's behavior. The individual must truly accept the goals (participative goal-setting), and each goal must be specific, measurable, attainable, realistic, and timely (SMART goals).
- Need theories (Maslow's Hierarchy of Needs, Alderfer's ERG Theory, Herzberg's Dual-Structure Theory, and David McClelland's Need Theory): Need deficiencies cause behavior.
- Expectancy theory: An individual's behavior is a function of three factors (expectancy, instrumentality, and valence). The expectancy factor refers to an individual's belief that effort leads to a certain performance level. The performance level is associated with a specific outcome (instrumentality factor), and the outcome is valued by the individual (valence factor).

Why are personality theories important?

What can be gained from the theories of personality is threefold. First, the various personality theories offer a framework for evaluating the extent to which a person believes that he or she is a worthwhile and deserving individual (self-esteem). Second, based on a person's self-esteem, an individual's actions and behaviors can be better understood. Third, embedded in an individual's personality is the rigidity of that person's beliefs (dogmatism) and his or her openness to other viewpoints.

Personality theories provide a glimpse into a person's beliefs about his or her capabilities to perform a task (self-efficacy), the degree to which an individual is willing to take chances and make risky decisions (risk propensity), and the extent to which an individual believes that power and status differences are appropriate within hierarchical social systems, including the cultural environment that an individual is exposed to.

Culture and Personality

Think of a cultural environment as a kaleidoscope of societal elements that swirl around, absorbing and influencing every individual—like the twisting winds of a tornado scooping up everything in its path. Specifically, a cultural environment consists of the attitudes and perspectives shared by a group of individuals, meaning that a unique society, as well as any possible subcultures, has been formed.

Life Experiences and Personality

Besides being molded by the societal fingers of the culture in which we live, the events of daily life also leave a unique mark on who we are and how we behave. In fact, the combination of culture and life experiences, such as our family environments, the location(s) where we grew up, the schools we attended, the work situations we encountered, our love relationships, and the friends we have chosen are probably responsible for 50 percent of our personality.

For some individuals, the experiences of daily life have left them bitter, so they view the world as a hostile, empty, and foreboding place, while for others the opposite is true. What's important for us to remember is that each of us must be aware of our power to positively or negatively affect the outlook of another person. Stopping to offer a few dollars to a homeless person for a meal at McDonald's or working at a charitable event may not alter the overall circumstances of someone who's struggling to survive, but the fact that a person is willing to help a less-fortunate person speaks a great deal about that individual.

In our quest to unmask our "true" essence and ultimately discover the path of life we have chosen to follow, we have so far explored perception and the elements of personality, including heredity characteristics, environmental factors (culture), and the influence of daily events.

Flowing from our perceptions and personality are the attitudes or opinions we have adopted. Understanding our attitudes brings us another step closer to revealing our inner being—our soul, if you like. As stated by Stephen Laws (1987), a horror novelist, "A man is what his thoughts are every day."

We all express our opinions about everything, from a coaching decision during a sporting event to what we think about another person to the quality or worth of a piece of art. Our opinions and attitudes may or

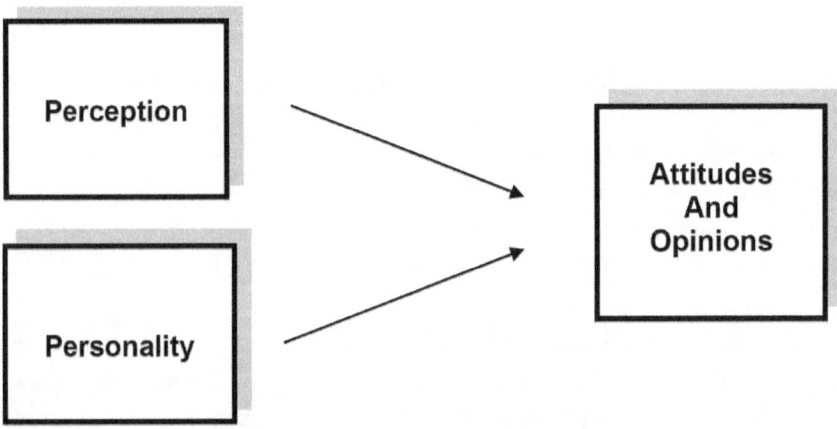

may not be based on facts, but every attitude is comprised of three components. The cognitive component is the opinion or belief segment of an attitude. The affective component is the feeling or emotional segment of an attitude. The behavioral component is an intention to behave in a certain manner toward someone or something.

Our opinions and attitudes affect our motivation to act in a certain manner. Motivation refers to a person's willingness to exert high levels of effort. Individuals are willing and able to exert a high level of effort when recognition is provided for accomplishments and when opportunities for advancement are available. A motivated individual sets the stage for a lifetime of success. Given today's competitive, global business environment, no individual can expect to achieve any degree of success in life without an internal drive to want to be a productive and self-reliant person. Furthermore, only productive, self-reliant individuals can motivate and lead others toward achieving extraordinary accomplishments and a fulfilling life.

In the end, a journey of self-discovery involves taking an internal peek at something we may not want to see and risk the possibility that we might need to change. Every human being has a perceived image of who they think they are, and any challenge to that belief is not something anyone tends to welcome. However, personal growth cannot occur unless we objectively journey into our psyche and thoroughly examine what makes us tick. As stated by Swimme and Berry (1992), "The story of the human is the story of the emergence and development of this self-awareness and its role within the universe drama."

Recall from previous statements, the essence of our inner being can be referred to as our self-concept. Our self-concept is an organization

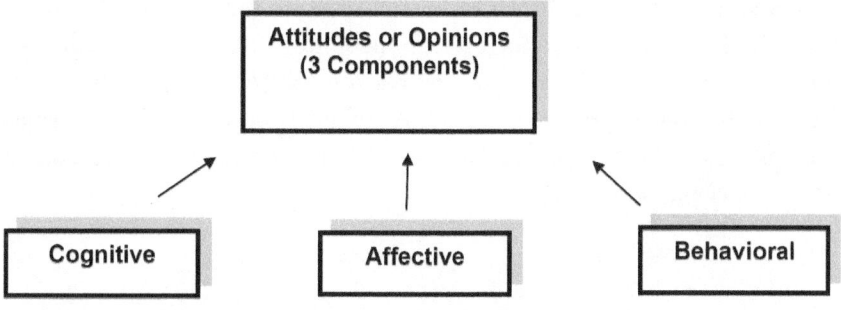

or patterning of attitudes, habits, knowledge, drives, and the like, all of which blends together to form our personality. Generally, we reflect on our self-concept as a result of some circumstances or one's own conscious introspection. This "self-examination is a preparation for insight—a groundbreaking for the seeds of self-understanding that gradually blooms into changed behavior" (Brouwer, 1964).

If during the self-examination an individual sees themselves in a way that they do not like, then that individual is changing their self-expectation. From a change in self-expectation, a new self-concept emerges. like a newborn hatchling breaking through the shell to experience the outside world for the first time. The change in self-concept must ultimately be self-directed—the individual must want to change.

- Attitudes and opinions affect motivational level.
- Only motivated individuals set the stage for a lifetime of success.
- Only motivated individuals can inspire others to be motivated.

In the final analysis, individuals are masters of their own destinies in the sense that they take charge of their personal development. Nothing can be done to individuals to make them want to grow; they will mature only if they have the desire and wherewithal to do so.

For many people, an internal voyage to the deepest regions of their self-concept may never occur, but for us the path that we have been following has been leading us toward an understanding of who we are while also revealing the path of life we have chosen to follow.

Looking beyond the mirror to see our true identity is one of the most difficult challenges that a person can encounter in life, but as a character in one of the books by Tamara Thorne (2004) states, "I guess my point is that there's never been a time when I didn't live for information, and I've always felt that, for me at least, learning and growing is the primary purpose of life."

WHICH PATH TO FOLLOW?

The ultimate quest for knowledge is discovering who we are. Don't be afraid to see, because only then can we change for the better.

At the end of the movie *High Plains Drifter*, as the leader of a notorious band of outlaws is frantically looking from side to side in the hope of spotting a fast-shooting, mysterious drifter, the villain shouts in a desperate, haunting tone, "Who are you?" As sweat drips down the face of the outlaw and fear fills his eyes, the only response from the drifter is a bullet that ends the villain's life. Hell is the next stop for the outlaw and quite possibly for the mysterious drifter, too. Fortunately for us, in our quest of self-discovery, we have not had to engage in a violent struggle between the forces of good and evil and the middle ground between those two extremes, but we have had to wrestle with the concepts of perception, personality, attitudes, and motivation. It's the mixing of those concepts that molds us into who we are—just like a sculptor chisels a piece of marble until the desired form is achieved. The end result for the sculptor is a work of art; the outcome for an individual is the recognition of the path in life they have chosen to follow.

Every person follows one of two paths in life: (1) a productive, self-sufficient path or (2) a dependency path. Imaginary economics tends to lead an individual on the dependency path and a life of economic stagnation. The intentions and numerous promises of imaginary economics are rarely achieved, and most often the final result for individuals on the dependency path is misery, envy, bitterness, and the desire to blame society for the situations they find themselves in.

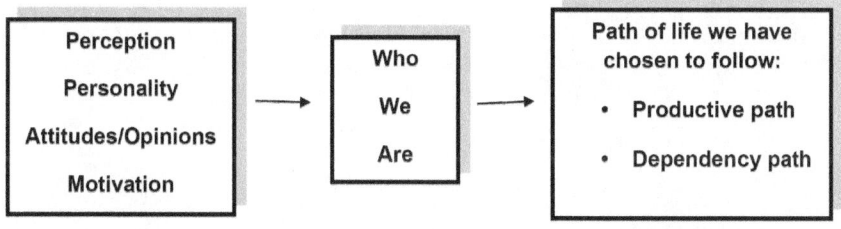

For those on the dependency path of life, their perceptions, personality, attitudes, opinions, and motivational influences have been shaped by the social and economic policies and programs established by economists, politicians, reporters, teachers, and academicians who promote the falsehoods of imaginary economics. The ideology of imaginary economics is a sad game that robs people of fulfilling lives.

However, the principles of real economics foster an economic environment in which a person's perceptions, personality, attitudes, and motivational influences are built around personal accountability, self-reliance, and the drive to be productive and successful. The picture is clear: To achieve a fulfilling life, the ideology of imaginary economics must be exposed.

SUMMARY

- Life consists of two paths: a dependency path or a productive, self-sufficient path.
- For those on the dependency path of life, their perceptions, personality, attitudes. opinions, and level of motivation are fundamentally influenced by the ideology and social and economic policies and programs of imaginary economics.
- For those on the self-reliant path of life, their perceptions, personality, attitudes, opinions, and level of motivation are fundamentally affected by the principles of real economics.

REFERENCES

Brouwer, P. J. (1964, November–December). The power to see ourselves. *Harvard Business Review, 42*(6): 156–165.
Crichton, M. (2002). *Prey*. New York: HarperCollins.
Laws, S. (1987). *The wyrm*. New York: Leisure Books.
Swimme, B., & Berry, T. (1992). *The universe story: From the primordial flaring forth to the ecozoic era: A celebration of the unfolding of the cosmos*. New York: HarperCollins.
Thorne, T. (2004). *Thunder road*. New York: Kensington, Pinnacle Books.

5

FACTS VERSUS OPINIONS

In today's culture, most individuals are long on opinions and short on facts. The reason facts have been pushed to the side is the ability of many individuals to blur the line between a fact and an opinion.

In the case of imaginary economics, the facts simply do not matter; what is important is the big-government ideology that motivates the believers. Facts tend to get in the way of the practitioners of imaginary economics. What counts is repeating the false social and economic promises of imaginary economics. It's like in the music business, when a song is played over and over on the radio: If the song is heard enough, it eventually becomes a hit. That's how the practitioners of imaginary economics operate: They repeat their myths over and over until the myths take on the appearance of being truths. For those individuals who do not know the facts, the repeated myths of imaginary economics are thought to be reality.

Those who promote imaginary economics are masters at turning myth into reality.

Being able to see through the various social and economic smoke screens of imaginary economics involves separating opinions from facts and unraveling myths from reality. But exposing facts from opinions is a difficult challenge for two reasons. First, many people do not want to see the facts, and second, the economists, politicians, reporters, teachers, and academicians who promote imaginary economics are skillful at twisting the facts so that confusion is created.

To uncover the deceit of imaginary economics, we must look further into the difference between facts and opinions.

To start unraveling facts from opinions, let's first understand that the knowledge-creation process stems from the definition associated with each academic discipline; just like the Big Bang gave birth to the universe, the definition of each academic discipline gives life to that academic discipline. The definition of an academic subject describes why the academic discipline exists:

- Physics is the science of matter, energy, and interactions between the two, grouped in such traditional fields as acoustics, optics, mechanics, thermodynamics, and electromagnetism, as well as in modern extensions, including atomic and nuclear physics, cryogenics, solid-state physics, particle physics, and plasma physics.
- Geography is the study of the features of the Earth and the distribution of life on Earth, including human life and the effects of human activity.
- Geology is the study of the Earth, the material of which it is made, the structure of those materials, and the processes acting on them.
- Economics is the social science that deals with the production, distribution, and consumption of goods and services at the macro and micro levels.
- Psychology is the study of human and animal behavior.
- Sociology is the study of social relationships, organization, and change.
- Mathematics is the science of using numbers and symbols to deal with quantities, forms, and their relationships.
- Astronomy is the study of celestial objects, space, and the physical universe as a whole.

- Organizational behavior is devoted to understanding, explaining, and ultimately improving the attitudes and behaviors of individuals and groups in organizations.
- Biology is the study of life and living organisms, including their structure, function, growth, origin, evolution, and distribution.
- Management is the study of the short-term and long-term activities of planning, organizing, staffing, and controlling the daily functions within an organization to achieve maximum outcomes in an effective and efficient manner. Within the field of management is the academic discipline known as strategic management planning, which focuses on the product choices and industry characteristics that affect the profitability and survival of an organization.
- Statistics is the science of collecting and analyzing data to learn about ourselves and our surroundings.
- Chemistry is the branch of science that deals with the composition and properties of substances and various elementary forms of matter.
- Educational leadership deals with applying management and leadership principles to the field of education.
- Oceanology is the study of the physical and biological aspects of the oceans.
- Medicine is the science and art of diagnosing and treating disease or injury and maintaining health.

Given the existence of these academic disciplines, how is learning propelled forward? Simply put, a body of knowledge is established. Think of a body of knowledge as the facts upon which each academic discipline is built. The goal of any student studying an academic subject is to understand the body of knowledge within that academic field. Those who grasp the body of knowledge become experts in that subject.

FACTS FROM VARIOUS ACADEMIC DISCIPLINES

- $2 + 2 = 4$
- H_2O is the chemical symbol for water.
- The diameter of the Earth is 7,926.41 miles.

- The sun is the closest star to the Earth, about 93 million miles away.
- The peak of Mount Everest is 29,035 feet above sea level.
- When a price increases, the quantity demanded decreases, ceteris paribus (the law of demand).
- When a price increases, the quantity supplied increases, ceteris paribus (the law of supply).
- Light travels at a consistent, finite speed of 186,000 miles per second.
- The Pacific Ocean is the largest and deepest of the world ocean basins.
- The oceans hold approximately 96.5 percent of Earth's water. Approximately 71 percent of the Earth's surface is covered with water.
- The Nile River is 4,258 miles long.
- Asia is the largest continent in the world.
- Higher taxes mean lower disposable income.
- The largest land mammal in terms of weight is the hippopotamus.
- The opening price of Walmart stock on June 17, 2015, was $72.63.
- The total assets of Microsoft amounted to $176.68 billion (2015).
- The three branches of the US government are the legislative, executive, and judicial.
- In 2011, the United States spent $11,841 per full-time equivalent (FTE) student on elementary and secondary education, an amount 35 percent higher than the Organisation for Economic Co-operation and Development (OECD) average of $8,789.
- The distance from the Earth to Mars varies because both the Earth and Mars are following elliptical orbits around the Sun and are traveling at different speeds. Sometimes the planets are close together, and at other times, the planets are on opposite sides of the Sun. The result is that the distance between Earth and Mars changes from minute to minute.

Moving from facts to opinions, I use three concepts: informed opinion, belief opinion, and challenge opinion. Recall from the previous chapter that a people's actions and behaviors are affected by their opinions and attitudes.

Three Types of Opinion

- Informed opinion
- Belief opinion
- Challenge opinion

People's actions and behaviors are affected by their opinions and attitudes.

An informed opinion is a statement based solely on the facts that have been established within the body of knowledge of an academic discipline, meaning that the statement has been accepted as fact by the majority of experts within the discipline.

A belief opinion is a statement that is consistent with a person's paradigm of the world. A belief opinion may be based on no facts, a misunderstanding of the facts or body of knowledge, a misinterpretation or misperception of the facts, a disregard of the facts, or the misrepresentation of facts for the sole purpose of implementing a course of action that supports a person's paradigm of the world—in other words, his or her ideology—to support what the individual believes to be true regarding a situation.

A challenge opinion is a legitimate questioning or challenge of the facts. This situation occurs when the overall body of knowledge or the facts about a topic within an academic discipline is being established or when the established body of knowledge in an academic discipline is being challenged. For example, Einstein's theory of special and general relativity challenged the notion of gravity, time, and space. Challenge opinions are a fundamental analysis tool for insuring that the body of knowledge in an academic discipline is accurate. The body of knowledge must be comprised of facts, not belief opinions.

The economists, politicians, reporters, teachers, and academicians who promote imaginary economics for the most part express belief opinions when discussing social and economic programs in order to create a gray area between the intentions of the programs and the facts or actual outcomes. Without this gray area, the falsehoods of imaginary economics would be easily exposed, and the ideology of imaginary economics would cease to exist.

The practitioners of imaginary economics promote their ideology through belief opinions.

Recall, that the practitioners of imaginary economics cherish their misguided big-government ideology more than anything else. Outcomes must be ignored when there is a mismatch between the intentions of the ideology and the actual results of the programs supported by the followers of imaginary economics.

Real economics is built on informed opinions or facts. The facts must guide all economic and political decision-making. Following the facts is the only way to truly help everyone achieve a reasonable standard of living. The economic facts are there; what's needed is the will to see the facts and expose the myths of imaginary economics.

SUMMARY

- Many individuals confuse facts with opinions.
- The economists, politicians, reporters, teachers, and academicians who promote imaginary economics take advantage of the confusion between a fact and an opinion to promote the falsehoods of imaginary economics.
- Never forget that it is the actual outcomes of social and economic programs and policies that are important, not the intentions.

6

MICROMANAGING NEVER WORKS AND USELESS POLITICIANS VERSUS USEFUL POLITICIANS

Micromanaging at the organizational level does not work, so why would it work at the societal level? The truth is, micromanaging at the societal level does not work, and therefore the promoters and practitioners of imaginary economics must ignore reality and create the illusion that big government and government control fosters social and economic success.

To unravel the foolishness that big government and economic prosperity are closely linked, let's recognize that it is private businesses and organizations that generate economic activity and growth. Governments are transfer entities that redistribute financial assets, physical capital, and human capital. This redistribution function distorts macroeconomic performance. The bigger the government, the bigger the economic distortion; a society whose economic engine is controlled by the government is a society in social and economic trouble. For example, think of the former Soviet Union; were waves and waves of individuals trying to enter and live in the Soviet Union? In fact, the Soviet Union had to build a wall to keep people from trying to escape, and that basically tells the whole story; government domination is a horrible way to live.

Government domination of a society is a horrible way to live. The former Soviet Union had to build a wall to keep people from trying to escape.

Do not get me wrong: There is room for government in society and the economy, but it is a limited place. Those who promote imaginary economics hide the reality that big government is counterproductive; government takes from Peter to pay Paul. Recall that the economists, politicians, reporters, teachers, academicians, and others in society who promote the ideology of imaginary economics are masters at creating a gray area between facts and opinions, where nothing grayish exists.

Let's take a step back and focus on the importance of private businesses and organizations within an economy. A key component of organizational sustainability is leadership. Unfortunately, a straightforward definition has proven elusive, for *leadership* has been defined in many ways:

- A process involving the use of noncoercive influences to achieve certain goals
- A set of characteristics that, when used effectively, can influence others
- The process whereby a person influences others to pursue a vision
- The process of guiding and motivating others to accomplish organizational strategies and objectives
- The ability to articulate a strategic vision or mission for an organization
- The ability to motivate others to buy into a vision
- The ability to influence others
- The ability to get other people to get the best out of themselves and achieve organizational goals
- The ability to develop others

And the list goes on and on, but the definition isn't important. What matters is that the right type of leader is in place, meaning an individual who pursues organizational goals and objectives in such a way that the growth and integrity of the employees are respected (Johnston quoted in Seyfarth, 1999). The specific characteristics of the right type of leader include:

- The right self-image and self-concept to create a workplace in which the traditional management–employee relationship paradigm is cast aside in favor of a new management–employee paradigm; employees are regarded as partners, not subordinates. Management must put employees first and mean it. Management retains the final decision-making authority, but the focus is on how an organizational decision affects the employees, for that in turn will influence how the employees perform their jobs and ultimately how they interact with customers.
- The ability to easily adapt to various situations. The right type of leader is sociable, conscientious, tactful, considerate, and open to various points of view.
- A focus on the conditions of all the individuals who work for them, not themselves. By truly caring about the employees, the right type of leader will achieve unparalleled organizational success. The right type of leader makes a true commitment to the employees, and it is that commitment that inspires the employees to want to accomplish organizational goals in the most effective and efficient manner (social exchange theory).
- The willingness to embrace change, whether it is small or large, whenever it is necessary to do so. In fact, the right type of leader actively promotes an organizational culture that has an enhanced capacity to learn, adapt, and change.
- An altruistic perspective on life. Only that kind of person has the characteristics to inspire others to want to do their best.
- A pursuit of organizational goals and objectives in such a way that the growth and integrity of people are respected.

Now let us compare the characteristics of a leader with a leadership style that flows from an egocentric perspective of life. This can best be described as a CREEP approach to leadership:

CREEPS are *control* freaks. CREEPS make all the decisions and exert only a token or superficial effort to seek employee input or suggestions. CREEPS are the ultimate micromanagers. Anything not initiated by CREEPS is rejected.

CREEPS form *relationships* with favorite employees. Work performance is secondary. Only those in the inner circle of CREEPS are allowed any involvement in the day-to-day managerial activities of the organization.

CREEPS have king- or queen-sized *egos* and view employees as easily replaceable cogs in a machine. CREEPS have very little or no concern for employees except for the CREEPS' favorite employees. CREEPS use HR policies to intimidate and severely limit employee empowerment.

CREEPS have limited *ethics*. CREEPS use a Machiavellian approach to accomplish tasks. CREEPS are abusive and manipulative. CREEPS are concerned only about themselves and view others as human pawns to be used as CREEPS see fit; any employee development only occurs if it benefits CREEPS.

CREEPS love *power* and institute a top-down managerial philosophy. CREEPS are not interested in developing future leaders because those individuals are viewed by CREEPS as threats. CREEPS love to show off their power.

CREEPS are as *secretive* as possible. CREEPS don't like to share information with employees. Employees find out information through the grapevine. When CREEPS must share information with employees, it is communicated through formal communication channels, and generally the employees are not allowed (or are only superficially allowed) to be part of the decision-making process.

The difference between the right type of leader and CREEPS is also illustrated by slightly modifying the work of Peters and Austin (1985). Characteristics of the right type of leader include:

- Is comfortable with people
- Puts employees first
- Is an open-door cheerleader
- Does not demand a reserved parking place, private washroom, or private dining room
- Has the common touch
- Is a good listener
- Is fair

- Is humble
- Is tough when confronting nasty problems
- Tolerates disagreement and is respectful of the opinions of others
- Has strong convictions (altruistic approach to life)
- Trusts people
- Gives credit and takes blame
- Prefers personal communication over written communication, such as memos, e-mail, and long reports
- Keeps promises
- Thinks that there are at least two other people in the organization who would be good administrators

The description of CREEPS includes:

- Are uncomfortable with people
- Put their own needs, not the needs of the employees, first
- Are generally inaccessible to employees
- Have reserved parking places, private washrooms, and dining areas
- Have strained relationships with employees
- Are good talkers in terms of outlining what they want but poor listeners otherwise
- Are fair to their favorite employees while exploiting the rest
- Are arrogant
- Avoid nasty problems and are elusive (artful dodgers)
- Do not tolerate disagreement or respect the opinions of others
- Do not stand firm but vacillate and use a Machiavellian approach
- Distrust employees and focus on numbers on reports
- Take credit and blame others for failures
- Prefer written communication over personal contact
- Do not keep promises
- Make sure that no one is hired who remotely resembles a qualified administrator (or a challenge to their authority)

In terms of organizational performance, which leadership style achieves maximum performance? I think it is obvious that the right type of leader can create a workplace characterized by highly energized, dedicated, and productive employees always willing to do their best.

CREEPS' leadership style will establish an organizational environment in which minimum performance is the norm.

An organization with the right type of leaders will outperform an organization filled with CREEPS because the right type of leaders can tap the full potential of the workforce.

Thus, a vital key to organizational success and sustainability is to fill leadership positions with the right type of leaders, meaning individuals who possess an altruistic approach to life and who focus on the needs of the employees. CREEPS must be eliminated from leadership and managerial positions to maximize organizational performance.

A Key to Organizational Success and Sustainability

Fill organizational leadership positions with the right type of leaders, meaning individuals who possess the "right type of leader" characteristics described in this chapter. CREEPS must be eliminated from any leadership and managerial position to maximize organizational performance.

Leadership and organizational success and sustainability are locked in an eternal struggle against the numerous forces that can devour an organization in today's highly competitive marketplace. The crucial role of leadership can best be summarized by the following story told by Dr. Ronald Walker during a graduate class at Jackson State University:

> You can learn a lot about leadership by watching a farmer trying to get a group of cows to move from one pasture to another. The farmer can get behind the cows and try to push them through one gate and into another pasture. Eventually the farmer will get the cows into the other pasture; however, he would have spent a lot of time and used a

lot of effort. Instead of trying to push the cows, the farmer could have observed which cow was the lead cow and placed a bucket of feed in front of that cow and easily, with minimum effort, led that cow, and subsequently the other cows, out of one gate and through another into a new pasture. However, what we must always be careful of is who has the bucket and where are they leading us; it could be to the slaughterhouse.

With the right type of leader, no one worries about the direction in which the organization is heading because management and the employees will mutually agree on that decision. Ultimately it is the values and character of the right type of leader (grounded within an altruistic approach to life) that foster the creation of a productive workplace characterized by motivated employees who are always willing to do their best. That is the kind of organization that will survive the rigors of the marketplace and achieve sustainability.

The notion of the right type of leader and CREEPS at the organizational level can be applied at the societal level using the terms *useless politician* and *useful politician*.

In the never-ending quest to improve economic performance, the economists, politicians, reporters, teachers, academicians, and others in society who promote the ideology of imaginary economics propose an assortment of social and economic redistribution programs supposedly aimed at economic advancement, much like puppies who race in circles trying to catch their tails. After all that frantic scrambling around, what emerges from those misguided efforts are, at best, short-term spikes in some economic performance numbers. Long-term social and economic solutions remain a mystery.

An Economic Reality

Steady, long-term economic results require more than being guided by the economic belief opinions of the supporters of imaginary economics.

Long-term social and economic activity will never be maximized while we continue to search for silver-bullet solutions and allow politicians to force their political agendas on the economic system. Injecting the ideology of imaginary economics throughout every aspect of society is the first characteristic of a useless politician. The useless politician does not care about economic outcomes but instead is primarily motivated by the desire to advance a political ideology, expand political power, and achieve the societal goals embedded within their political ideology.

The useless politician talks a lot about the equality and importance of outcomes but never examines what outcomes are being achieved. All the useless politician focuses on is the intentions of his or her policies, not the actual outcomes. To the useless politician, the outcomes are generally ignored or, worse, lied about because the outcomes for the most part don't support the intentions. The useless politician lives in the world of false intentions, never in the world of reality, because reality and facts shatter the illusionary intentions.

The Useless Politician

The useless politician lives in the world of false intentions, never in the world of reality and facts, because the facts shatter the illusionary intentions.

Because the useless politician is so fully indoctrinated in the political ideology of imaginary economics and blinded by the glittery intentions of the ideology, the useless politician never freely admits that he or she has made a mistake or that his or her political philosophy and policies are imperfect. On the rare occasions when the useless politician is forced to admit that a mistake occurred, the mistake is minimized, and the admission is usually communicated in such a way that leaves the situation murky so that blame can be easily passed around. As the blame game heats up, the true nature of the mistake and subsequent outcomes are hidden under layer upon layer of confusion and deception.

In fact, the useless politician thrives at deception and acts like a magician using sleight-of-hand tricks and other actions to cover up the facts or divert attention from the outcomes of a policy or political ideology. By the way, major policy blunders are never fully acknowledged by a useless politician because to accept the fact that a major mistake has occurred threatens the foundation of the imaginary economics ideology. Above all, in the eyes, heart, and mind of a useless politician, the political ideology of imaginary economics must never be questioned.

The Useless Politician

The useless politician is an artful dodger, and above all else, the political ideology of imaginary economics must never be questioned.

Another strategy for a useless politician is attacking successful and productive individuals because successful and productive individuals do not need useless politicians. Useless politicians need individuals who are dependent on the policies and actions of the useless politician. This creates a false sense of the importance of politicians and their governmental policies.

The message and political actions of the useless politician are focused on convincing individuals that the main, if not only, reason they are not successful is because of the individuals who are successful and productive. Let's be clear: Being productive is the key to increasing the probability of a successful life, not dependency on the government. The useless politician creates dependency for the most part.

Being productive means that an individual has valuable knowledge, skills, and abilities to lead a fulfilling life. Individuals who decide to be productive increase the probability of living a more successful life than individuals who decide to be mediocre or worse; a truly great society fosters the notion of being productive, not being dependent on government programs. Being productive and self-sufficient is not the message the useless politician wants individuals to hear.

Being productive and self-sufficient is not the message that useless politicians and the other supporters of imaginary economics promote.

The bottom line is that the promoters of imaginary economics want control over the economic system and foster policies and programs that discourage people from striving to be productive and self-sufficient. Much like CREEPS diminish organizational performance, the useless politician promotes government dependency and limits economic opportunities. To the useless politician and the other promoters of imaginary economics, it's all about control at the individual and societal levels.

On the other side of the coin are useful politicians and the supporters of real economics. These individuals understand that economic growth stems from social and economic freedom, not the heavy hand of big government.

SUMMARY

- Micromanaging at the organizational level and big government at the macroeconomic level will never achieve maximum economic outcomes.
- Useless politicians and the other supporters of imaginary economics are all about micromanagement and big government.
- Useful politicians and the other supporters of real economics understand that economic growth occurs within a framework of limited government and when individuals are free to pursue their own economic interests.

REFERENCES

Peters, T., & Austin, N. (1985). *A passion for excellence*. New York: Random House.
Seyfarth, J. T. (1999). *The principal: New leadership for new challenges.* Upper Saddle River, NJ: Prentice-Hall.
Walker, R. (2007, Spring). Class lecture at Jackson State University.

Part Three

The Schizophrenic World of Economics and Teaching Choice in Economics Education

7

ECONOMIC WAY OF THINKING

To put it simply, productivity is the foundation for economic growth. Individuals and societies that are productive have a higher standard of living than unproductive individuals and societies. Does anyone want to leave a highly productive society to live in an unproductive society? If we are honest, the answer is no. To be more specific, who would rather live in North Korea than the United States or Canada or Germany or any democratic country? No rational person is willing to risk her or his life to enter North Korea or any other country under the control of a totalitarian government. Totalitarian governments are characterized by limited economic opportunities, low personal incomes, shortages of goods and services, and minimal productivity levels.

Countries with a totalitarian government are horrible places to live.

Productivity, scarcity, incentives, decision-making, and opportunity costs are fundamental concepts of the academic discipline of economics. All economists are initially taught to use the economic way of thinking to understand the world. However, many economists eventually lose their focus, forget their training, and unfortunately support political policies that violate the fundamental principles on which economics is based. The political lure of the "best intentions" of a public policy or program ultimately draws some economists away from the "reality of the outcomes" of the policy or program. Like Darth Vader being pulled to the dark side, the "best intentions" economists finally become no better than useless politicians.

Some economists are no better than useless politicians.

To useless politicians, the economic way of thinking represents a threat to their political views because it focuses on the independence of an individual, not dependency. Useless politicians are primarily concerned with their status, and this grows with dependent—not productive and independent—citizens. Thus, useless politicians must attack success and being productive. How often do you hear useless politicians blame successful individuals for the lack of success of others? The attack on success is part of the artful dodge of useless politicians because it diverts attention from their policies, which are the root cause of many social problems.

The Useless Politician

The useless politician promotes dependency on government and not being productive and self-sufficient.

People lead a meaningful life through personal accountability for decisions, not blaming others for one's failures; working hard; supporting a limited, effective government; and striving for excellence. Dependency on the policies, programs, and actions of useless politicians is the pathway to nowhere. Recall the statement attributed to Jesus: "You can give a man a fish, and he will eat for a day, but teach a man to fish, and he can eat for a lifetime." The useless politician is only interested in giving a man a fish so the man will always need the useless politician.

ECONOMIC WAY OF THINKING

The best way to help individuals become successful and lead a meaningful life is to turn away from the ideology, policies, and programs of the useless politician. The focus for achieving a fulfilling life must be on the fundamental components of the economic way of thinking.

A fulfilling life is not achieved by the ideology, policies, and programs of the useless politician but instead by focusing on the fundamental components of the economic way of thinking because the economic framework encapsulates the real world, not some utopia.

THE ECONOMIC WAY OF THINKING AND REALITY

The first economic reality is the notion of scarcity, the idea that the material desires of consumers outstrip the factors of production, or the input variables required to produce goods and services. In other words, the longing for goods and services is greater than the ability to produce the goods and services. Therefore, production decisions must be made. We cannot have everything we want, thus decisions become an important aspect of life. From a societal perspective, every society has had to come to grips with three economic questions: What goods and services do we produce? How do we produce the goods and services? Finally, who receives what has been produced (a distribution issue)?

Scarcity, decisions, and three economic questions societies must address: what to produce, how to produce it, and who receives it.

Linked with decision-making are the economic realizations of opportunity costs and the impact of incentives on the decision-making process. An opportunity cost reflects the economic reality that, with every decision to do or get something, something else is given up or sacrificed. In other words, to get more of something, something else must be reduced; getting more of A results in less of B.

In addition, any decision is influenced by incentives; if a positive incentive is put forth, then an individual will respond in a positive manner, and a negative incentive will invoke a negative response. Policy makers must always be aware of the incentives of a policy. The key question involving policy-making should be whether the policy will make an individual more productive or less. Only policies that make a person more productive should be instituted.

If the goal is to help a person achieve a fulfilling life, then social and economic programs must promote personal accountability, increase productivity, and help an individual to become self-sufficient.

Given scarcity and the consequences of making decisions, we return to a fundamental dilemma that must be faced in life: Does an individual choose to be productive and live a meaningful life or take the path of dependency?

The useless politician conveys a message that, if one's life is less successful, then it is the fault of successful individuals or the various organizations or institutions within the society or, frankly, anything else other than the choices that the individual has made. This deceitful ploy by the useless politician is quite successful and fosters the notion of dependency and entitlement and, for the most part, twists the economic way of thinking inside out.

The policies, practices, and actions of the useless politician develop a "victim mentality" that permeates every corner of the society, destroying the notion of personal accountability, just like cancer erodes a healthy body. It is a sad cycle of poverty that the useless politician creates for many in society, but the useless politician can always point the finger at some other source.

> The useless politician is the root cause of social and economic problems.

Given all the individual and social problems that the useless politician creates, how can we spot a useless politician and, as the slogan goes, "vote the bum out of office." The answer is rather straightforward. First, do not be deceived by how useless politicians presents themselves because they specialize in putting on a good show; everything they say will sound good.

Once we put the show aside, focus on the policy statements and ask one question: Does that policy provide an incentive to be productive? If the answer is no, then you have uncovered a useless policy, and if the politician generally advocates policies that do not support being productive, then you have unmasked a useless politician. We can call this the Milton Friedman test because he always tried to convey that it is the outcome of a policy that is important, not the intentions.

Milton Friedman Test

Used to detect useless politicians and useless social and economic policies and programs

Now that we have uncovered a way to identify useless politicians and the useless social and economic ideology they peddle, our eyes can see how we are diverted by the intentions of social and economic policies rather than focusing on the outcomes of policies. Frankly, it boils down to what useless politicians value above anything else, and that is status and power.

The useless politician is always trying to control everything in society, and the results are usually mediocre at best.

To the useless politician, the economic system, like every other facet of life, must be controlled from the top down. The social and economic policies and programs must be in tune with the ideology of the useless politician, which is a philosophy that promotes the blame game, us against them, and the "victim mentality." This unhealthy trinity seeps into the fabric of society as the useless politician blames the economic system for the social and economic problems people encounter. Personal accountability has little or no place in the social and economic policies and programs of the useless politician.

The useless politician focuses on creating the "unhealthy trinity":

1. The blame game
2. Pitting people against each other
3. Creating the "victim mentality"

As always, the useless politician is the master illusionist who opens the door to policies that appear to have merit but only foster mediocre social and economic outcomes. But that's par for the course with useless politicians. Thus, it is now clear that, to help individuals achieve a fulfilling life, the first step must be to overcome the useless politician.

The bottom line is there is no place in society for useless politicians and their policies and programs.

Using the characteristics of the useless politician, we can now describe a useful politician. Basically, the useful politician is the exact opposite of the useless politician. Useful politicians understand that the economic way of thinking is reality, and they support social and economic policies that encourage productivity, self-reliance, and personal accountability.

The Useless Politician versus the Useful Politician

The useful politician understands that fostering dependency on government programs has nothing to do with being compassionate or helping the poor. Dependency is about achieving political power and placing the politician above the rest of society. The useful politician promotes independence from the government and supports policies that promote individual and societal productivity because that leads to a satisfying life.

In short, the useful politician focuses on (1) promoting the dynamics of demand and supply with limited and efficient government and (2) measuring the success of government programs by the outcomes achieved. Those achievements include economic growth; a reduction in government dependency; and private-sector job growth, especially small business development.

The useful politician is the exact opposite of the useless politician.

Which politician would better serve society: the useless politician or the useful politician? The answer is obvious; therefore, the only question is, Why would anyone support useless politicians?

SUMMARY

- The economic way of thinking is focused on scarcity, incentives, decision-making, personal accountability, and opportunity costs.
- The economic way of thinking leads to the conclusion that productivity is the foundation of economic growth.
- A society (and individual) that is productive gets more; a society (and individual) that is not productive gets less.
- Useless politicians (and some economists) ignore the economic way of thinking and instead promote social and economic policies that create the "unhealthy trinity": (1) the blame game, (2) pitting people against each other, and (3) the "victim mentality."
- If the societal goal is to help an individual lead a fulfilling life, then there is no place in society for useless politicians and their social and economic ideology.
- The useful politician is the opposite of the useless politician.

REFERENCE

Friedman, M. (1975, December 7). Interview with Richard Heffner on *The Open Mind*.

8

IMAGINARY ECONOMICS VERSUS REAL ECONOMICS

Beneath the stars lies our everyday world, a world seemingly far removed from the forces that guide the universe, a world for the most part uninterested with the mysteries and wonders of the cosmos that surround us, an earthly world controlled by the economic forces that shape the lifestyle of every human being.

Economists grapple with understanding the economic forces that surround society, forces so dynamic that they can lift an individual's standard of living to a higher plain or bring a person tumbling down to the lowest financial valley. Like a boat being tossed up and down by large and small waves, economic activity gains strength and then falters, leaving in its wake many financial successes and failures.

Economic forces affect everyone in society.

The role of money in a society, government intervention in the business community, poverty, distribution of income, profit maximization, supply and demand, international competition, productivity, labor–management relations, limitations of natural resources, inflation, recessions, government taxing and spending, interest rates, consumer spending, investment spending, and wealth creation are only some of the economic factors that exert a powerful influence on society.

As shifting economic forces push and pull societies in various directions, each person within the society experiences an array of feelings. Eventually, the positive or negative economic feelings generated at the individual level spread across the entire society, much like how a stone tossed into calm water creates a series of ripples across its once-smooth surface. During negative economic cycles, anxiety, doubt, and even despair can spring forth as a society is propelled toward a seemingly unpredictable and uncontrollable economic future. When the economy is moving in a positive economic direction, feelings of financial security and optimism abound.

The upward and downward movements of the economic forces that affect the economy are important because everyone is concerned with earning a living and tapping into the goods and services that are produced. Individual economic successes and failures affect a people's self-image and their role in society. Economic prosperity and equality of opportunity are the seeds that bring forth a politically stable society, where each person has an opportunity to reach personal and professional goals through hard work.

A prosperous economy creates political stability.

Besides the impact on our daily lives, we are often intrigued by how the different economic variables come together in the marketplace and produce an economic environment in which no member of society can escape. The economic environment, or economy, that engulfs a society can be described as a manmade entity that consists of all the income and production generated within a country.

Figure 8.1 illustrates that, within every economy, the production of goods and services must equal the income generated from the production of those goods and services. Businesses produce the goods and services that are available within a society, and households purchase those goods and services. Households provide businesses with the factors of production, and in return households eventually receive all the

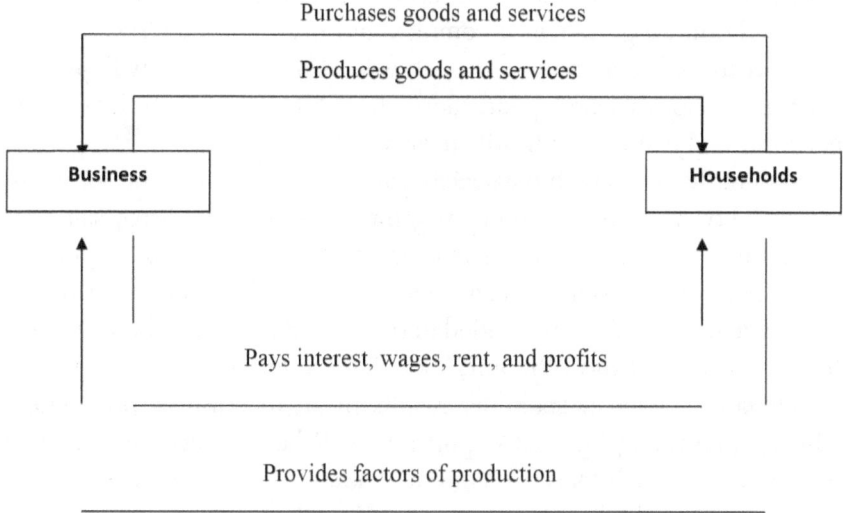

Figure 8.1.

interest, wages, rent payments, and profits distributed. Therefore, production equals income, and it is the link between production and income that determines the financial strength of an economy.

In today's world, the economy of each country affects the economic performance of every other country. Thus, the world economy resembles a patchwork quilt, in which the economies of every country are woven together and form one giant economic community.

The relationship between national and international economic phenomena and the lifestyle that an individual can obtain forms the centerpiece around which our lives are structured.

Because economic growth and production are so vital to a society, the health of the economy is constantly monitored for signs of strength and weakness. When the economy is strong, it serves as a lifeline that keeps a society together. When the economy is weak, it can act as a fuse that sets off an explosion of social unrest. Because of the connection between economic performance and social stability, economics and politics are bound together in a complex and often difficult relationship. The mixture of economics and politics is a courtship that will last forever as economists and politicians attempt to gain control over the economy and maintain authority over society.

Economic forces within a society can foster an atmosphere of financial stability when the economy is growing, wages are rising, sales are expanding, productivity is increasing, and technology is advancing. These positive economic signals create a feeling that our lives, from an economic perspective, are headed in the right direction. When a society feels secure about the economy, spending on goods and services tends to increase. A rise in spending results in an increase in production, which expands employment opportunities. When the economy is in an upward cycle, individuals feel confident about their economic situations and tend to have high expectations regarding the future.

On the flip side, economic forces create anxiety when the economy falters, unemployment spreads throughout every sector of the economy, inflation climbs higher, consumer purchasing power is reduced, sales decline, and production decreases. Thus, a downward trend in economic performance reduces confidence in the economy. People start to worry about their jobs and wonder if their income will be enough to cover their expenses. Individuals cut back on spending, which reduces production and increases unemployment.

When the economy is in a downward cycle, political finger-pointing intensifies, and social unrest starts to boil to the surface, threatening the structure of society. If economic performance continues to deteriorate, the societal threads that hold a community together may come undone. Eventually, the society will collapse and fade into history.

The ups and downs of economic activity not only cause concern but also can easily create confusion over what is occurring within the economy. One of the main problems that economists face in forecasting economic conditions is that the economy is in a constant state of flux and the data required to complete an analysis cannot be quickly collected. The lack of accurate and timely data makes the task of economic forecasting a risky business.

Another problem with economic forecasting is that economists cannot create a laboratory to examine cause-and-effect relationships among the various economic variables. Thus, the inability of economists to place an entire economy under a microscope causes a research void that hinders the ability of economists to accurately and consistently predict economic events.

How can we obtain permanent economic growth? How can we manage inflation? What is the key to increasing productivity in the manufacturing and service industries? How do individuals determine how much of their income to spend or save? What role should the government play in the economy? Can the economy be controlled? What role does money play in economic growth? How are prices determined? What type of economy can help the most people? We begin our exploration of these questions with the suggestion that the field of economics needs to return to its roots in the social sciences. In fact, it is the moral issue of how to help each person achieve a fulfilling life that divides imaginary economics from real economics.

The economists, politicians, reporters, teachers, academicians, and other followers of imaginary economics believe that a fulfilling life is achieved through big government, in other words, socialism and redistribution of wealth and income. The supporters of real economics realize that economic freedom and the decisions that individuals make in life steer a person toward a fulfilling or disappointing life. Ultimately, it is what's in a person's soul, their attitudes, motivational levels, behaviors, and actions that affect their success or failure. Collectively, we can refer to this as the "soul of mankind" or the "soul of a society."

Productive societies produce more goods and services, create more employment opportunities, and therefore have more financial and other resources available to help the needy.

Your lifestyle, my lifestyle, everyone's lifestyle is influenced by the economic system adopted by the society. The more an individual becomes familiar with the forces that affect the workings of an economic system, the greater the probability that he or she will be able to improve their quality of life and have a positive impact on others in the society.

Because our lifestyle depends on achieving "economic prosperity," our daily routines and many of our actions are driven by economic considerations. Because the economic realities of daily life exert such a powerful influence on every individual, a more in-depth understanding of economic principles may also lead us toward a deeper understanding of ourselves and the society in which we live.

To further our journey into the realm of economics, just like a group of explorers seeking out the unknown, let's start with the statement that the field of economics is a social science rather than a natural science. The natural sciences (also known as the physical sciences) investigate nature and the properties of material bodies and natural phenomena. The social sciences focus on investigating social phenomena, so social sciences are concerned with studying and analyzing human behavior.

Economics is a social science.

Thus, the social sciences, for the most part, are not governed by the physical laws of nature. As a result, the social sciences have not been able to establish explanatory generalizations that yield precise predictions like the theories of the natural sciences.

Because economics is a social science, the economic phenomenon that is studied pertains to man-made forces that are not subject to the physical laws of nature. Does the inability to base economic theory on physical or natural laws mean that economics research and theories are meaningless? Of course not, because it is only through research and the development of theories that a field of study can move toward the discovery of truth.

Research uncovers facts that lead to the discovery of additional facts. Through this discovery process, the building blocks of knowledge are compiled. As knowledge increases, mankind moves toward an understanding of the universal truths that shape our economic world. To uncover these truths, economic theories are developed on a macro- and microlevel.

Macroeconomics is concerned with the problems of economic growth, unemployment, and inflation. Each of these factors is an indicator of the overall state of the economy and how fully resources are used. By law, in the United States, the government has a macroeconomic responsibility for ensuring that economic growth remains high and that unemployment and inflation remain low. Through fiscal and monetary policies, the government of the United States attempts to achieve these economic goals. Monetary policy involves regulating the amount of money in circulation within an economy. The federal reserve is responsible for monetary policy. Fiscal policy relates to the taxing and spending policies of the government.

Macroeconomics: fiscal and monetary policy

Microeconomics is concerned with individual products and decisions made by individual firms and consumers. Microeconomics digs beneath the macroeconomic picture to understand how economic activity occurs on an individual basis instead of a societal or aggregate analysis.

Microeconomics: understanding what happens beneath the macroeconomic level

Both macroeconomic and microeconomic principles are rooted in a chain of reasoning that begins with the concept of scarcity. Recall from a previous chapter that scarcity refers to the premise that all resources are limited (scarce) while demands are unlimited. Because of scarcity, choices must be made, and trade-offs exist. To produce more of one good or service requires lowering the production of another good or service. Economists use a production-possibilities frontier to measure the amount of production that must be sacrificed of a good or service when the production of another good or service is increased.

---〰️---

Economics is based on the concepts of scarcity, choices, and trade-offs.

---〰️---

Scarcity and production choices are best illustrated by the fundamental economic concepts of demand and supply. In a free-market society, economic decisions are determined by individual preferences in the marketplace; in other words, demand and supply govern economic outcomes. If there is a strong demand for a good or service, then that good or service will be produced or supplied. A higher demand for a good or service leads to an increase in the quantity supplied of that good or service as the short-run price increases. The purchase price establishes the monetary value associated with a good or service.

Money can be thought of as a commodity that plays several crucial roles in an economy; for our purposes, I focus on its role as a medium of exchange, meaning money can be traded directly for other commodities. Sellers are willing to take money in exchange for their product or service, with the knowledge that, as buyers, they can freely exchange the money for other commodities.

Money is the economic lubricant that keeps the financial engine of an economy running, and most of our daily routines are devoted to earning the money necessary to purchase the goods and services we desire. The more value (or importance) a society associates with an occupation, the more money (income) an individual can receive. The more income, the more goods and services an individual can afford. The more goods and services produced, the higher the production level for society. Thus, the demand for and supply of goods and services drive production in a free-market society. Production then generates employment, which provides the income that individuals use to purchase the goods and services that are produced.

Through demand and supply, an equilibrium price (also known as the market-clearing price) is eventually established in the marketplace, meaning that the price an individual wants to pay for a good or service will be the exact price that eliminates any shortage or surplus of a good or service. Thus, the price and quantity demanded and supplied of a good or service are said to be in an equilibrium state. The equilibrium price auction model in figure 8.2 illustrates an equilibrium state.

A supply curve is a graph of a supply schedule. It shows how the quantity supplied changes as the price changes, holding all other determinants of supply constant for a specific time frame. A demand curve is a graph of a demand schedule. It illustrates how the quantity demanded changes as the price changes, holding all other determinants of demand constant for a specific time frame. The equilibrium price represents the price at which the quantity demanded by consumers equals the quantity supplied by suppliers.

The most effective way to achieve equilibrium price and quantity is through the free market, where competition among producers leads to an equilibrium state. Competition forces producers to provide products at the price and level of quality demanded by the consumer.

Although the equilibrium price auction model is the best model for understanding the economic activity of a society, the clarity that the equilibrium price auction model brings to the world of economics is turned upside down by the economists, politicians, reporters, teachers,

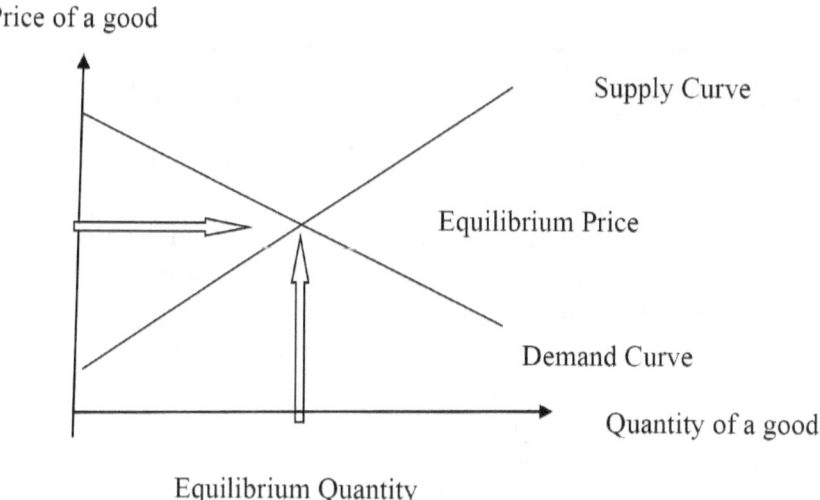

Figure 8.2.

academicians, and other followers of imaginary economics. The *Alice in Wonderland* world of imaginary economics based on the intentions worldview creates the schizophrenic behavior so often demonstrated by economists. The intentions of economic and social programs are noble, but it is the outcomes that matter. Thus, the boundary between imaginary and real economics begins with a focus on intentions or a focus on outcomes or results.

The difference between imaginary economics and real economics:

- The intentions worldview of economics → imaginary economics
- Results-oriented worldview of economics → real economics
- Intentions of economic and social programs might be noble, but it is the outcomes or results that matter.

To further diagnose the schizophrenic world of economics, several other variables can be used to clearly separate imaginary economics from real economics.

CHARACTERISTICS OF IMAGINARY ECONOMICS: THE INTENTIONS OF POLICIES, NOT THE OUTCOMES

- Imaginary economics are government-focused (practitioners of imaginary economics can never have enough government departments, programs, regulations, taxes, and so forth). As stated, handouts from the government is the fundamental belief of those who practice imaginary economics, and unfortunately for those trapped within the clutches of imaginary economics, economic dependency on the government is the outcome.
- Socialism is the underlying political philosophy, meaning extensive government involvement in all aspects of the society, including the production and distribution of goods and services, or, in other words, centralized economic power. A centrally planned economy exists

when the government primarily decides how economic resources are allocated, not the marketplace. Keep in mind, the economists, politicians, reporters, teachers, academicians, and other followers of imaginary economics never or rarely refer to the word *socialism* because doing so would expose their economic and social motivations and undermine their ability to implement their economic and social agenda.
- Another aspect of socialism is the political ideology of income and wealth redistribution. Socialists are always seeking to redistribute income and wealth from those individuals who produced the income and wealth to those who have not worked to produce the income and wealth. The more an individual believes in socialism, the more redistribution of income and wealth is promoted. Unfortunately, income and wealth redistribution eventually reduce productivity, which lowers output and ultimately decreases income. Socialists and practitioners of imaginary economics ignore the economic reality of continual income and wealth redistribution because the ideology of socialism and imaginary economics is what is important. Economic facts and reality must be ignored so the ideology of imaginary economics can flourish.
- Socialists and practitioners of imaginary economics extensively use belief opinions to spread economic and social myths and create a gray area between economic facts and reality.
- Socialists and practitioners of imaginary economics focus on micromanaging the economy and many aspects of society.
- Socialists and practitioners of imaginary economics rarely focus on results or outcomes of economic or social policies and programs and always push the intentions (or ideology) of the policies or programs; this violates the Milton Friedman rule—economic and social policies and programs should be evaluated according to the results or outcomes of the policies or program, not the intentions.
- Socialists and practitioners of imaginary economics ignore Albert Einstein's statement about insanity because the followers of imaginary economics always want more of the same policies and programs. As a matter of fact, that's the primary reason given when their policies and programs do not work; the program only needs more money or more government control or more income and wealth redistribution or more time for the various economic and social programs to

become effective. The practitioners of imaginary economics never run out of excuses for policy or program failures.
- Socialists and practitioners of imaginary economics focus on giving a person a fish so the person depends on the government instead of teaching a person to fish so the person can be self-sufficient.
- Socialists and practitioners of imaginary economics extensively use the blame game to pit people against each other and create the victim-mentality scenario. Practitioners of imaginary economics actively promote the unhealthy trinity.
- Socialists and practitioners of imaginary economics diminish the importance of personal accountability and being productive.
- Socialists and practitioners of imaginary economics ignore the fundamental components of the economic way of thinking, especially the reality of opportunity costs and trade-offs, meaning to get more of something, something else must be sacrificed.

―――∞―――

Among the followers of imaginary economics are useless politicians.

―――∞―――

CHARACTERISTICS OF REAL ECONOMICS: THE RESULT OF ECONOMIC AND SOCIAL POLICIES

- There are limited and effective government departments, programs, regulations, and so forth. If a government department, program, or regulation is not achieving the stated goals and does not increase productivity, then the department, program, or regulation should be terminated. As stated, the role of the government is to provide an economic hand up, not dependency on the government through its handouts.
- A market economy is the underlying economic philosophy, meaning that the decisions and actions of households and organizations in the marketplace determine the allocation of economic resources. The role of government is to enforce contract law and property rights and

establish effective and efficient regulations and remedies for any wrongs that are committed.
- Followers of real economics extensively use informed opinions because real economics is based on economic facts and the economic way of thinking.
- Micromanaging an economy never or rarely works.
- Followers of real economics always focus on results or outcomes of economic or social policies and programs. They do not violate the Milton Friedman rule: Economic and social policies and programs should be evaluated according to the results or outcomes of the policies or program, not the intentions.
- Followers of real economics do not violate Albert Einstein's statement about insanity because they understand that, if an economic or social policy or program does not achieve the proposed result or outcome, then that policy or program must be terminated.
- Followers of real economics focus on teaching a person to fish so he or she will not be dependent on the government; in other words, they teach a person to be self-sufficient.
- Followers of real economics discourage the unhealthy trinity of the blame game, pitting people against each other, and the victim-mentality scenario.
- Followers of real economics promote the importance of personal accountability and being productive.
- Real economics are based on the fundamental components of the economic way of thinking, especially the reality of opportunity costs and trade-offs, meaning to get more of something, something else must be sacrificed.

Among the followers of the characteristics of imaginary economics are useful politicians.

SUMMARY

- Economic performance affects every member of a society.
- A productive society produces more goods and services, creates more employment, and therefore has more financial and other resources available to help the needy.
- A society based on the ideology of imaginary economics will not be a productive society.
- A society based on the principles of real economics will be a productive society.

9

CHOICE AND ECONOMIC EDUCATION

Real economics deals with economic facts flowing from the economic way of thinking. Imaginary economics stems from the political ideology of socialism, or government control over society. Socialism is the breeding ground for the useless politician.

Because real economics is connected to economic facts and reality, the end results are higher productivity and more opportunities to enhance everyone's standard of living. The ideology of imaginary economics ends in economic stagnation. Economic decay through imaginary economics, or prosperity through real economics?

The best way to help others is to become productive yourself. Productive people generate financial assets that they can use to help others become productive. Productive societies and individuals are generated when the characteristics of real economics are embedded in the fundamental philosophy and practices of the society.

Now that the distinction between imaginary economics and real economics has been illustrated, there is still the unresolved issue of what economic educators should communicate to students and, at a macro-level, the public, as well as how the information should be communicated.

ECONOMIC EDUCATION

Our world is subject to a basic truth: Scarce resources set against unlimited wants creates a situation in which choices must be made. However, despite the reality of this fundamental economic condition, students tend to shy away from learning about economics. This trend is unfortunate because a solid foundation in economics will help students to better understand who they are and the business world that surrounds them.

Among the reasons students avoid economic courses is that, to understand economics, they need to be able to think in an abstract manner and to apply abstract concepts to economic situations. Students also need to be able to express complex ideas in a logical and straightforward manner. In sum, many students just view economics as a difficult subject. Given this perception, we must confront a crucial issue: If economic educators are truly interested in promoting economic education, then an examination of the teaching process and the communication exchange between teachers and students must be given more priority.

Students have different learning styles or preferences for dealing with intellectual tasks, as well as different practical, creative, and analytical abilities. To make sure that students from all social classes and cultural groups have an equal opportunity to learn in the classroom, economic educators must understand that they must use a variety of teaching methodologies, including:

- The collaborative problem-solving (CPS) approach has two components: problem-based learning and collaborative learning. Problem-based learning involves presenting students with a problem scenario. The students then work together in a collaborative effort to solve the problem. Collaborative group work fosters the development of improved communication and teamwork skills.
- Service-learning links academic coursework with community-service projects to improve each student's self-worth and foster an appreciation of teamwork. As part of the service-learning project, students are expected to identify economic issues, explore economic theories, and provide evidence relating their experiences to economic theories. The foundation for service-learning began

with the work of John Dewey (1938), who argued that, when students tended to the welfare of others, their lessons learned provided not only an educational stimulus but also an expansion of their horizons and encouragement to take responsibility for their fellow human beings (McGoldrick, 1998).
- McGoldrick (1998) and Becker and Watts (1995) suggest that the lecture method is the primary teaching methodology used in introductory economics courses. Lecturing has its place in a teacher's repertoire; however, to maximize student learning, the lecture method must not be exclusively used.
- Good lecturing in combination with student-centered leaning activities or active student participation offers a positive learning alternative to the straightforward lecture method. The student-participation component can consist of many variations, including picking a student at random during a lecture and then asking that student to paraphrase or comment on what was just stated. Other suggestions involve placing students into groups and having each group orally review the content of each lecture. The groups then submit a written summary to be compiled into a course-review document. Another method is the "minute paper," which is assigned in the last minutes of each class. Each student is required to respond to two questions: (1) What was the most important thing you learned in class today? and (2) What question(s) are unanswered? Other forms of the traditional lecture combined with a student-centered learning activity include (1) lecture discussion, (2) lecture and laboratory experience, (3) lecture recitation, (4) lecture with problem sets, and (5) lecture demonstration.
- Role-play simulation, such as "The Summit of the Americas," a macroeconomic simulation in which students play the part of representatives negotiating trade agreements on behalf of their respective countries. This simulation challenges students to process information efficiently, apply economic analysis, sharpen decision-making skills, and improve negotiation skills. A future dimension of the simulation could include groups of students from various countries using video-conferencing communication (Truscott, Rustogi, & Young, 2000).
- The inverted classroom approach moves activities that have traditionally occurred inside the classroom outside, and vice versa. For

example, lectures can be viewed outside of the classroom on a DVD or through some other communication technology, while end-of-chapter questions usually assigned as homework can become the focal point within the classroom.
- Case studies examining a variety of economic situations can be used.
- Technology-based teaching methodologies, such as DVDs, CDs, computers, and the internet, can promote student academic success and understanding of subject matter.
- Experiments, demonstrations, and dramatizations can effectively communicate economic concepts to students. A simple experiment can consist of holding an auction for a product or service. Bidding can begin at a certain price and increase at predetermined increments. A simple graph of the data would provide the students with a demand curve for the product or service. A more complex experiment can consist of making peanut butter and jelly sandwiches with only one knife in a fixed time frame. A production function can be derived from starting with one student, then having additional students participate, and then graphing the number of sandwiches produced against the units of labor. This experiment can illustrate the law of diminishing marginal returns (Lage, Platt, & Treglia, 2000).

BRINGING EVERYTHING TO A CONCLUSION

Now that numerous teaching methodologies have been outlined, it is time to return to the schizophrenic world of economics: imaginary economics versus real economics.

Not only are effective teaching methodologies a crucial component of economics education, but we must also decide what is being communicated.

As stated in this book, as well as in every introductory-economics textbook, economic analysis flows from the principles of the economic way of thinking. Imaginary economics generally ignores the economic way of thinking and is nothing more than a political ideology focused on government control. Imaginary economics might belong in the field of political science but not economics. The teaching of economics, no matter which teaching methodology is used, must cling to the principles of the economic way of thinking.

Only the practitioners of real economics incorporate the economic way of thinking into economic and social policy analysis.

For teachers of economics, the choice should be clear. The political ideology of imaginary economics has no place in economics. Teaching and communicating the economic and social realities embedded in real economics must become the priority in economics education.

SUMMARY

- An effective teaching methodology improves the learning process, and is that not the primary objective of economics educators?
- If the goal of the practitioners of economics is to truly understand how an economy can maximize individual and societal financial outcomes, then economics education must be based on the principles of real economics; there is no other choice.

REFERENCES

Becker, W. E., & Watts, M. (1995, October). Teaching tools: Teaching methods in undergraduate economics. *Economic Inquiry*, 33(4), 692–700.
Dewey, J. (1938). *Experience and education*. New York: Collier Books.
Lage, M. J., Platt, G. J., & Treglia, M. (2000, Winter). Inverting the classroom: A gateway to creating an inclusive learning environment. *Journal of Economic Education*, 31(1), 30–43.
McGoldrick, K. (1998, September). Service-learning in economics: A detailed application. *Journal of Economic Education*, 29(4), 365–376.

Truscott, M. H., Rustogi, H., & Young, C. B. (2000, December). Enhancing the macroeconomics course: An experiential learning approach. *Journal of Economic Education*, *31*(1), 60–65.

SUMMARY

Concluding the Issue

For each statement, answer true or false.

1. An individual will become more productive when government handouts are provided.
2. Bigger government is preferred over limited government.
3. Government programs and departments use resources in an effective and efficient manner.
4. Income and wealth redistribution should be a priority.
5. Government programs are an effective way to increase economic growth.
6. More government control over an economy is preferred to limited government control.
7. Politicians are more ethical than business leaders?
8. Individuals are unsuccessful in life because the economic environment favors the rich.
9. The government responds to individual needs better than corporations or other business organizations.
10. Economists believe that the outcomes of a government program match the intentions of the program.
11. The principles of real economics do not reflect economic reality.
12. Market outcomes cannot be trusted; only government programs can be relied on to be fair and provide equitable outcomes.

13. Government programs are needed to reduce the influence of the rich on income generation and business opportunities.
14. The economic way of thinking is not logical.
15. Businesses are only interested in profits and capturing market share for their products or services, while the government focuses on the welfare of its citizens.
16. A government program is preferred to a market outcome.
17. The government can be trusted.
18. Business leaders must be carefully monitored and regulated by government.
19. Businesses are not trustworthy.
20. Government programs are preferred to the supply and demand outcomes that occur in the marketplace.
21. The principles of real economics are just opinions.
22. The rich are the reason for social problems.
23. Government planning should be the core of any economic philosophy.
24. Economics education should focus on the benefits of government-sponsored economic activity.
25. An individual is unsuccessful in life not because of his or her decisions but because the economic environment favors businesses and the rich.
26. Serving in government is preferred over becoming a CEO.
27. Businesses are generally the cause of recessions.
28. The results of government programs reflect the intentions of the program.
29. Government should direct economic activity, not marketplace outcomes.
30. Politicians are better role models than business leaders.
31. The intentions of government programs should be stressed in economics courses.
32. Government fiscal policies help to control the negative aspects of the business cycle.
33. The economic way of thinking is not a realistic examination of fundamental economic principles.
34. Businesses are not responsible for their financial success because it is the fiscal programs of the government that are responsible for business and economic success.

35. Government central planning is essential for economic growth.
36. Individuals are forced to make decisions in life because the economic environment favors businesses and the rich.
37. The rich should pay for all government programs.
38. The principles of real economics should not be taught.
39. Individuals make poor decisions because the economic environment favors big corporations.
40. The notion of scarcity in economics is a false premise.
41. Economic problems occur because the rich have too much.
42. Outcomes of government programs match the intentions.
43. Government programs rarely create dependency.
44. Government regulations have a positive impact on economic growth.
45. Individuals need government programs because the economic environment favors businesses and the rich.
46. The ideology of imaginary economics is preferred over the economic way of thinking.
47. A centrally planned economy results in a higher level of gross domestic product.
48. Taxing the rich promotes economic growth and lowers government dependency.

Believers in the ideology of imaginary economics will respond true to most of these statements. This response illustrates the misguided ideology of imaginary economics. The only path toward economic prosperity for each member of a society is by following the realistic principles of real economics. Just examine the countries in the Economic Freedom Index. At the bottom of the index are countries like Cuba, North Korea, and Venezuela. These countries are perfect examples of the negative consequences of following the myths embedded in imaginary economics.

WALLS AND ECONOMIC OUTCOMES

The former Soviet Union needed to build a wall to keep their citizens from escaping. Government control and central planning created horrible living conditions for the people living in the various countries under the control of the Soviet Union. On the other side of the coin, countries that embrace a limited government and market outcomes need walls to keep people from illegally entering the society. Which society would you want to live in: the one where everyone is trying to escape or the one where everyone is trying to get into?

Government control brings misery. Imaginary economics is all about government control. What rational individual would want to follow the myths of imaginary economics?

SUMMARY

- Imaginary economics ends in misery.
- Real economics leads to economic prosperity.
- Which economic path do you want to be on?

ABOUT THE AUTHOR

Daniel Wentland is the *author of Reality and Education: A New Direction for Educational Policy; Knowing the Truth about Education; Organizational Performance in a Nutshell;* and *Strategic Training: Putting Employees First.* His articles have been published in the *Ivey Business Review, Compensation and Benefits Review,* and *Journal of Education*—the oldest educational journal in the United States.

www.ingramcontent.com/pod-product-compliance
Lightning Source LLC
Chambersburg PA
CBHW022016300426
44117CB00005B/221